The
Great American
GOLD
R·U·S·H

ALSO BY RHODA BLUMBERG

Commodore Perry in the Land of the Shogun
The Incredible Journey of Lewis and Clark
The First Travel Guide to the Moon

The Great American GOLD RUSH

by Rhoda Blumberg

Bradbury Press   New York

I am indebted to James P. Ronda, professor of history, Youngstown State University, who scrutinized the manuscript for accuracy and assisted me with his expert advice.

I am also grateful to Grace Evans, curator of the history department at Wells Fargo Bank in San Francisco, and George Miles, curator of the Western Americana Collection at the Beinecke Rare Book and Manuscript Library, Yale University, for helping me locate many of the illustrations in this book.

Bradbury Press
An Affiliate of Macmillan, Inc.
866 Third Avenue, New York, NY 10022
Collier Macmillan Canada, Inc.

Printed and bound in the United States of America
First Edition
10   9   8   7   6   5   4   3   2   1

The text of this book is set in 14 point Bembo.
Maps by Paul J. Pugliese

LIBRARY OF CONGRESS CATALOGING-IN-PUBLICATION DATA
Blumberg, Rhoda.
The great American gold rush / by Rhoda Blumberg.
p.   cm.
Bibliography: p.
Summary: Describes the emigration of people from the East Coast of
the United States and from foreign countries to California
to pursue the dream of discovering gold.
ISBN 0–02–711681–6
1. California—Gold discoveries—Juvenile literature. 2. Voyages
to the Pacific Coast—Juvenile literature. 3. Overland journeys to
the Pacific—Juvenile literature. 4. California—Description and
travel—1848–1869—Juvenile literature. [1. California—Gold
discoveries. 2. Voyages to the Pacific Coast. 3. Overland journeys
to the Pacific. 4. California—Description and travel—1848–1869.]
I. Title.   F865.B6524 1989   979.4′04—dc19
89-736   CIP   AC

FOR JERRY
and our family

Larry, Robin, Rena, Alice, David, Leda, Tom

Daniel, Carla, Ilana, William, Melodica, Gregory,
Amalia, Dana, Eliza

TABLE OF CONTENTS

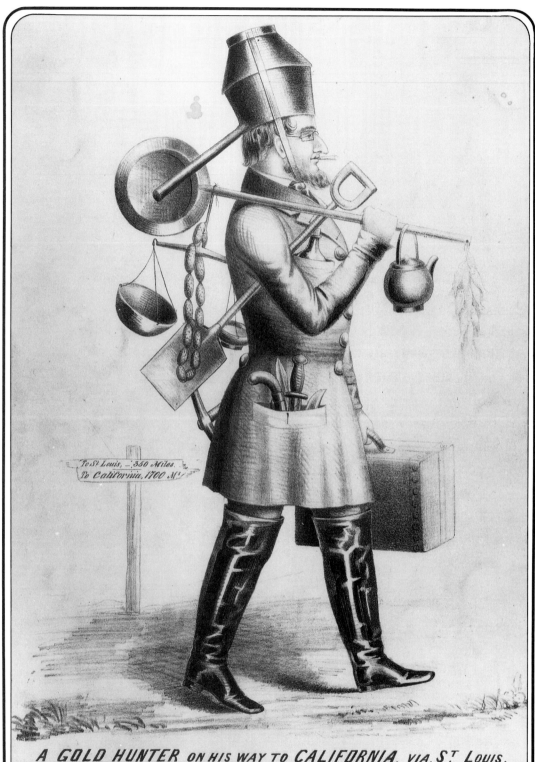

To St Louis, 350 Miles.
To California, 1700 M.

A GOLD HUNTER ON HIS WAY TO CALIFORNIA, VIA, St LOUIS.

Published by H.R.Robinson, 31 Park-Row, N.York

1 · GOLD FEVER

STREAMS PAVED WITH GOLD! Glittering nuggets loose on the ground, scattered everywhere! No machinery needed. A pick, shovel, pocketknife—even a kitchen spoon will do. Free for the taking, no government restrictions. Stake a claim, collect the loot, and carry home a fortune.

After its discovery in 1848, gold in California was said to be as common as clay. The yellow metal was a magnet that pulled people from all over the world. They seemed possessed, drawn by a force too strong to resist. Thousands left their families, shut their shops, deserted their farms, and headed for the West. Newspapers called them victims of "gold mania," or "gold fever."

The fever was highly infectious. It affected the brain and caused delirious dreams. Sergeant James Carson, for example, envisioned piles of gold, castles of marble, thousands of slaves bowing to him, and a multitude of maidens vying for his love. Others with less vivid imaginations hoped to pay off mortgages, start new businesses, or just loaf in luxury for life.

Before 1848, California was a thinly populated, unimportant Mexican province. Farms and cattle ranches dotted vast expanses of land. Settlements along the coast were occupied by traders who supplied wood and water for ships and sold cowhides and tallow to merchant vessels. During the 1840s, Oregon Territory was the goal for thousands of homesteaders, who were attracted by reliable reports about its fertile soil. Only a few hundred pioneers made their way to Mexican California.

The United States acquired California and other western lands on February 2, 1848, when the Treaty of Guadalupe Hidalgo was signed in Mexico after the Mexican War (1846–1848).[1] The signers of this treaty weren't aware that gold had been discovered in California just a few weeks before. They never imagined the land held riches that would disrupt the lives of thousands of people all over the world and cause one of history's great migrations.

It started with a nugget no bigger than a dime, found at John Sutter's sawmill. Sutter was a bankrupt shopkeeper from Switzerland. He had deserted his wife and five children in 1834, fleeing to America to avoid paying debts. This strange, complex man tried to carve a career for himself in

Sutter's fort in 1847

THE GREAT AMERICAN GOLD RUSH

Missouri, New Mexico, Oregon, Hawaii, and Alaska, but failed.[2] His luck changed when he came to California in 1839. Sutter was able to impress Mexican officials by faking his past. Posing as a former captain for King Charles X of France, he hoodwinked them with his affectations. The Mexican government granted him fifty thousand acres of land in the Sacramento Valley. Since the land was in a remote wilderness, his holdings weren't considered valuable.

"Captain" Sutter, convinced that he owned a private empire, swaggered about as lord of a domain, which he named New Helvetia. ("Helvetia" was an ancient name for Switzerland.) American pioneers, European immigrants, workers from Hawaii, and native Californians helped him develop his land. Local Indians were his "peasants," his "subjects." As laborers, they erected buildings and cultivated his fields. The Indians were no drain on Sutter's purse. Their wages consisted of clothing and beads and other baubles. They ate their meals kneeling over troughs of food, and they were locked up each night so that they couldn't escape to their tribal homes.

Until 1848, Sutter prospered. Using borrowed money, he bought herds of cattle, horses, and sheep. He turned his land into huge wheat fields, vineyards, and fruit orchards. On a slight rise near the Sacramento River, he built Fort Sutter. Its fortified walls were guarded by uniformed sentries. The fort served as his headquarters. It had shops, a flour mill, tannery, distillery, blanket factory, and quarters for workers and guests. Sutter's fort dominated the Sacramento Valley. As the "capital" of New Helvetia it attracted pioneers, many of them enchanted by their host's charm.

Sutter strutted about with a bodyguard of Indians who were part of his private army. He boasted that he had "the largest military force ever assembled in the north"[3] and that he had the power of life and death over Indians and whites in New Helvetia. This lord of the Sacramento Valley even

John Sutter

James Marshall

minted his own coins: small circles of metal, each stamped with a star—tin, not gold.

Sutter never dreamed that treasure was hidden in the earth. He expected to become rich through farming and trade, and he wanted more and more people to settle and work in his domain. Lumber was always needed to build up his empire. He made a contract with a carpenter named James Marshall to set up a sawmill. Marshall chose a site about forty-five miles east of the fort, on the American River, in the foothills of the Sierra Nevada mountains, and the men set to work.

One day in January Marshall noticed a yellow metal "about as much as a ten-cent piece would hold."[4] It was shining in the millrace (a channel for water that drives a mill wheel). *Gold* registered in his brain. To test it Marshall banged the nugget with a stone. It didn't shatter. Then he had the camp's cook place it in boiling lye. It didn't tarnish.

Marshall brought the metal to Sutter, who looked up the entry for "Gold" in the *American Encyclopedia,* then conducted the tests recommended. When Sutter applied nitric acid, the metal didn't corrode. When he weighed it, the nugget was heavier than silver.

It was gold; no question about it.

Instead of being elated, "Captain" Sutter was upset. He didn't want his workers distracted from their jobs, and he certainly didn't want strangers invading his property and digging it up while hunting for treasure. Sutter told the mill workers to keep the discovery secret and to stay on the job until the mill was finished. They agreed not to tell anyone, probably because they didn't want competition from others. But the mill workers looked for gold after working hours, and they found that the point of a knife could scrape it from the river's bank—a bank with small amounts of hard currency in the form of yellow flakes.

A secret of such brilliance was bound to radiate. Even Sutter couldn't resist bragging. In a letter to a Mexican neighbor, written only two weeks after Marshall's discovery, he said, "I have made a discovery of a gold mine which, according to experiments we have made, is extremely rich."[5] The driver of a supply wagon returned from the sawmill with a nugget. When he used it to buy liquor at a store in New Helvetia, gold began to cast its magic spell.

Within six weeks, workers at New Helvetia had quit their jobs and headed for the hills. Hides and grains were left to rot in storehouses, and the finished mill on the American River lay idle.

When news about the gold discovery reached the small, sleepy town of San Francisco, nobody seemed impressed. Reports of gold usually turned out to be false alarms. This short item, on the back page of the newspaper *Californian*, dated March 15, 1848, downplayed the discovery:

> GOLD MINE FOUND.—In the newly made raceway of the Saw Mill recently erected by Captain Sutter, on the American Fork, gold has been found in considerable quantities. One person brought thirty dollars worth to New Helvetia, gathered there in a short time. California, no doubt, is rich in mineral wealth; great chances here for scientific capitalists. Gold has been found in almost every part of the country.[6]

The *Californian*'s rival newspaper in San Francisco, the *Star,* casually mentioned gold as "an article of traffic." But by May it told readers that the gold story was fake: "all sham—a superb take-in as was ever got up to guzzle the gullible."[7]

Sutter's Mill

However, men who wanted to check out the story went to the American River and returned carrying pouches of gold. The *Star*'s owner, Sam Brannon, is said to have whipped up a frenzy by running through the streets of San Francisco waving a bottle filled with gold dust he had collected near Sutter's Mill. According to a popular tale, he shouted, "Gold! Gold! Gold from the American River." Brannon also had a store that sold mining equipment. By making news, he might have been promoting his own interests.

San Francisco caught gold fever. Starting in May 1848, the town went crazy. Doctors, lawyers, bakers, blacksmiths, laborers—all left town to prospect for gold. Officers and entire crews deserted ships in the harbor.[8] The town's two newspapers folded: no staff. Churches shut their doors: no congregations. The mayor and other government officials took off. Even the sheriff left to seek his fortune. By summer most of the men had left town.[9]

The news spread south to Monterey, California, on May 29, 1848. The Reverend Walter Colton, the town's diary-keeping mayor, sent a scout to inspect various diggings, and when the scout returned with pockets filled with gold, there was hysteria. Colton reported, "All were off to the mines, some on horses, some on carts, and some on crutches; and one went on a litter."[10] Colton complained that there were no servants left. "The millionaire is obliged to groom his own horse, and roll his wheelbarrow [and] . . . clean his own boots." The situation was especially shocking for Rev. Colton because he had to make his own breakfast "in a smoking kitchen grinding coffee, toasting herring, and pealing onions!"[11] He felt especially sorry for himself after meeting men who had found one hundred thousand dollars' worth of gold. One lump weighed over twenty pounds. Colton left town and headed for the hills.

Like San Francisco, Monterey practically closed down.

Nuggets the size of
boulders were
featured in this
French cartoon.

Sailors and soldiers joined the mass march to the mines. Colton's diary reports that "three seamen ran from the [United States warship] *Warren,* forfeiting their four years' pay; and a whole platoon of soldiers from the fort left only their colors behind."[12] Army records show that within eighteen months, 716 soldiers of a total of 1,290 had deserted their posts in California. A private whose pay was six dollars a month could hardly resist the get-rich-quick opportunity.

California's military governor, Colonel R. B. Mason, issued a proclamation asking civilians to capture deserters. However, few gave chase. People were too busy making their own arrangements to bother about arresting others. So many sailors jumped ship and so many soldiers were on the run that the commander of the United States Pacific Squadron wrote to the secretary of the navy in Washington that "for the present . . . and for the years to come, it will be impossible for the United States to maintain any naval or military establishments in California . . . for they [the enlisted men] would immediately desert."[13]

Tales of treasure travel well. By summer, ships had carried the news to Hawaii and returned to California packed with passengers. Settlers from the Oregon Territory headed south by sea or by covered wagon. The newspaper the *Oregon Spectator* stated that by the end of 1848 "almost the entire male population had gone gold digging in California."[14] This was probably an exaggerated report, but it does indicate that people were leaving in droves. When gold fever spread across the border to Mexico, thousands left home and traveled north to the promised Land of Opportunity.

South Americans pack to leave for gold country.

Many prospectors dug up glittering prizes in 1848. They found gold not only along the American River but also along countless other rivers and streams, and on hills and mountains. Edward Gould Buffum, an army lieutenant who was stationed in California, rushed to the gold mines as soon as his regiment was dismissed. He hoped to find "a fountain head of El Dorado, where, gushing in a rich and a golden lava . . . a stream of molten gold should appear before our enraptured eyes."[15] According to popular belief, there were gold veins hundreds of miles long and wide. Prospectors had only to scratch the surface to uncover yellow metal underfoot—an inexhaustible supply, enough for everyone, and anybody could find some easily. No need for scientific instruments or divining rods. California dirt was rich!

By the end of 1848, news about California gold reached South America, Australia, and Asia. Thousands set sail.

Americans living east of the Mississippi River didn't join the Rush of '48. Although there were tales about gold in the West, no one took them seriously. Faraway lands usually breed legends and exaggerations. Although letters from successful miners had been featured in newspapers during 1848, these were read as believe-it-or-not items—entertaining, but not to be taken seriously. Most people thought of California as a distant territory where Mexicans, "wild Indians," and a few trappers and traders lived. They became excited only after official reports were issued from Washington, D.C.

In June 1848, Thomas O. Larkin, the United States consul for northern California, wrote to Secretary of State James Buchanan that he had seen pure gold being dug by crowds. He said that shovels ordinarily worth one dollar were selling for from five to fifty dollars. He was convinced that prospecting could continue for one hundred years.

Larkin's report was accompanied by gold samples that were delivered to Washington, D.C., in September by his messenger, Lieutenant Edward F. Beale. Beale appeared

Panning for gold

President James Polk

before the Senate. The gold he brought was displayed at the Patent Office, where crowds viewed it and newspaper reporters raved about it. But the gold was seen as a curiosity. A discovery in a faraway territory didn't seem relevant to Easterners' lives.

Then in November, another report and more gold samples arrived. These were sent by California's governor, Colonel Mason, who reported that men at the diggings were averaging twenty-five dollars a day; that he saw two men dig up seventeen thousand dollars' worth in a short time; that hundreds of rich ravines were still untouched. "Gold is so abundant," he wrote, "that for the present there is room enough for all . . . the laboring man wants nothing but his pick and shovel and tin pan."[16] Mason's only fear was that gold could lose its value: It might become such a common metal that the world economy would collapse!

Two hundred thirty ounces of the gold that the governor had packed in a Chinese tea-leaf box were displayed at the War Department.

President James Polk delivered his Message to Congress on December 5, 1848. He said, "The accounts of the abundance of gold . . . are of such extraordinary character as would scarcely command belief." Polk assured everyone that reliable officials had told him "the supply is very large."[17] The president's speech had an astounding effect. It resulted in a raging epidemic of gold fever.

THE GREAT AMERICAN GOLD RUSH

2 · THE FEVER SPREADS

AFTER THE PRESIDENT'S SPEECH was publicized, wealth seemed guaranteed. Would-be treasure hunters went into such a frenzy that the New York *Express* reported, ". . . never were people so worked up . . . this last gold news has unsettled the minds of even the most cautious and careful among us."[1] Horace Greeley, editor of the New York *Tribune,* proclaimed "The Age of Gold" and predicted that within four years, miners would extract "One Thousand Million of Dollars."[2]

Now reports from the diggings were read avidly. It was impossible to stay calm when one newspaper wrote about men opening up a vein of gold "just as coolly as you would a potato hill,"[3] and another stated that California "gold is unbroken and extends over a tract 120 miles in length and seventy miles in breadth."[4] People everywhere clamored to join the grab for riches, anxious to get going quickly so they could be ahead of others and claim bonanzas first.

It would have been ideal to pack and leave for the West at once. But the great gold flap hit the East during winter. Overland travel was impossible until snows melted and spring grass provided food for horses, mules, and oxen. Nevertheless, those infected with gold fever couldn't wait.

Sea travel was an alternative to trekking across the country. An ocean voyage seemed quicker than waiting for

CALIFORNIA!
Mutual Protection
Trading & Mining Co.

Having purchased the splendid, Coppered and very fast Sailing

Barque EMMA ISIDORA,

Will leave about the 15th of February. This vessel will be fitted in the very best manner and is one of the fastest sailing vessels that goes from this port.

Each member pays 300 dollars and is entitled to an equal proportion of all profits made by the company either at mining or trading, and holds an equal share of all the property belonging to the company. Experienced men well acquainted with the coast and climate are already engaged as officers of the Company. A rare chance is offered to any wishing a safe investment, good home and Large profits.

This Company is limited to 60 and any wishing to improve this opportunity must make immediate application.

An Experienced Physician will go with the company.

For Freight or Passage apply to 23 State Street, corner of Devonshire, where the list of Passengers may be seen.

JAMES H. PRINCE, Agent,
23 State Street, corner of Devonshire St., Boston.

For further Particulars, see the Constitution.

spring, then hiking through wilderness and climbing over mountains. East Coast whalers and merchant ships frequently looped around South America's Cape Horn and headed up the California coast. This route usually took six to nine months.

Instead of the long route around South America, there were shortcuts involving two sea voyages and a land crossing. Easterners could choose the Panama route and hope to arrive in California in a few weeks. Or they could cross from the Atlantic to the Pacific by traveling across Nicaragua or Mexico.

Posters about oceangoing vessels were attached to city walls and country fences. Newspapers featured huge advertisements about ships with fine accommodations, superb food, and experienced crews at bargain rates. Holiday cruises to the Land of Plenty! All sorts of boats embarked from Atlantic and Gulf Coast ports.

The rush to get going

An 1849 cartoon, possibly inspired by Rufus Porter

Rufus Porter, editor of the *Scientific American,* offered an uplifting option. He had designed a flying machine, which he hoped would carry passengers to California in three days.

His "aerial locomotive" was to be propelled by a steam engine—a back-up safety feature, in case winds weren't blowing in the right direction. Its wood frame, covered with waterproof cloth, was also "arrowproof" against attacks by Indians. Passage: two hundred dollars per person. However, to entice customers, a gala inaugural trip was cut-rate: "Passage, $50, wines included. Baggage extra."[5] At least two hundred people signed up, but the trip was canceled after Porter realized that his project couldn't get off the ground.

To prepare gold-seekers for their great adventure, newspapers advertised items for miners. There were rifles, knives, and pistols—for protection against robbers and "wild Indians." Money belts designed for holding nuggets sounded exciting. Also, lace sold by the yard made elegant, fine sieves for sifting gold-flecked dirt. Cumbersome contraptions and complex gold-washers were featured as good buys. One

THE GREAT AMERICAN GOLD RUSH

Heading for California

GOLD MINES
OF
CALIFORNIA!!

W. R. ANDREWS,

Having just returned from California, after having spent several months in the mines and mountains of that interesting country, will deliver a

LECTURE,

at   day of   on   **1849,**

upon the GOLD MINES OF CALIFORNIA, and give a narrative of his journey to California, a description of the route and of the different places on the route to San Francisco, interesting incidents, &c. together with a full and accurate description of San Francisco, San Rafel, Benetia, Pacific New York, Mission Doloros, San Jose, Sutters' Fort, Suttersville, Sacramento City, Stockton, and many other places in California, of the bays, rivers, navigation, trade, mines, minerals, animals, vegetable productions, manners and customs of the miners and traders, government and laws, the Indians, &c., manner of digging and washing gold, amount procured by different individuals and many other interesting facts relative to California. He will also exhibit

GOLD DUST,

as found by the washers, and lumps as found, weighing from half an ounce to a half pound, with a model of the machines manufactured and used by miners to separate the gold from the soil and rock.

LETTER.

The undersigned, passengers in the steamer Panama, from San Francisco, Alta California, to Panama, having been informed that it is the intention of their fellow passenger, Capt. R. Andrews, of the state of New York, to deliver a lecture or lectures, upon the Gold Mines of California, on his arrival in the United States, take pleasure in recommending him, (from our acquaintance with him and his business,) alike in California,) to our Fellow Citizens, as a person well acquainted with the Country and Mines, and is probably better able to give correct information in relation to them than any other person of our acquaintance.

ANSON HOUSE, of   ...   late of San Francisco,
WHIT D. CONGABT, Macon, Ga.   do.
HOWARD ACKERLY, Brooklyn, N. Y., late of San Francisco,
Junk Morrison, Wood's Diggins & Sacramento city,

ARCHIBALD SINCLAIR, late of San Francisco,
John VOORHEES, Wood's Diggins, California,
GEORGE CROGAN, Mormon Diggins,
GRIFFITH ROWE, New York city, late of Corsus's Diggins.

On Board Steamer Panama, June 2?, 1849.   ROCHESTER DAILY ADVERTISER PRINT

bargain was a grease guaranteed to gild anyone from head to foot. Just follow the instructions: Rub it on your body, roll down a hill, and "gold and nothing else will adhere."[6]

The word *California* was everywhere. People danced "The San Francisco Waltz," "The Gold Digger's Waltz," and "The Sacramento Gallop." They sang "Oh Susannah" with these lyrics: "Don't you cry for me, I'm bound for California with a washbowl on my knee."

Whenever gold was mentioned, people were all ears. Speakers posing as experts lectured in sold-out auditoriums. Professor Boynton of West Point predicted that there would be gold in California for at least one thousand years. Mr. Atherton, another self-proclaimed authority, said that miners were making one thousand dollars a day, and that a mere handful of dirt could yield half an ounce of pure gold. Preachers were ignored when their sermons warned against the evils of easy wealth and the immorality of deserting family responsibilities.

Although there were a few reliable guidebooks based on the experiences of trappers, traders, and a trickle of pioneers who had gone west, the best-sellers were guidebooks hastily written by authors who had never left home. *The Gold Regions of California,* by a New York reporter, was better than most, because it included information from government reports. The author was realistic enough to warn readers that mining was hard work. But then he assured them that any man in fit condition could collect enough for his old age and leave "a handsome legacy" to his children. *California: Her Wealth and Resources* filled most of its pages with songs—and not a note of good sense. *Three Weeks in the Gold Mines,* by Henry Simpson, who claimed to have been at the diggings, made sensational reading. The author described picking up chunks of pure gold, one of them "as large and as thick as my double hand outspread." He told of an Indian who gladly exchanged a lump of gold for a red sash, and he described a streambed of solid gold that could be flaked away with a pickax. His book, which also gave advice about "the Best Methods of Getting There, Living Expenses, etc. etc.," sold for twenty-five cents—twelve and a half cents, half price, if you didn't buy his map. (A half cent was common change at that time.)[7] Gullible readers depended upon the book and his worthless map. One person who considered himself a skeptic said that he would be satisfied if he collected only "a hatful of gold a day."[8]

Four Months Among the Gold-Finders in California was another bogus guide, purported to be the memoirs of Dr. J. T. Brooks, who told about collecting a fortune in gold dust which, unfortunately, was stolen. This best-seller was translated into German, Dutch, French, and Swedish. "Dr. Brooks" was the product of a British writer's imagination.

Guidebooks of this sort were useless, misleading, and dangerous. Their exaggerations, mythical geographies, and bad advice deluded many who took these books with them when they headed west.

Most California-bound gold-seekers joined companies. In some instances, friends organized their own groups. The Old Harvard Company, for example, consisted of twenty-five college students. Large companies with more than one hundred people usually found participants through newspaper ads. Four hundred seventy-nine members made up Arkansas's Fort Smith and California Emigrating Company. All members paid the same fees and expected equal shares of the profits. Men mortgaged their homes, sold their belongings, and borrowed money. Many who could not afford membership dues found others to bankroll them in exchange for a percentage of their profits. Some companies purchased ships which they expected to sell after they docked. Getting home was a minor problem to be solved after the company members collected their loot.

Companies going overland or embarking by sea were often organized like military units. Members chose captains and lieutenants to lead others and drill them in the use of rifles, swords, pistols, and cannons. There were uniforms for dress occasions. One formal outfit included a cap trimmed with lace—a fancy fashion, not suitable for digging in dirt.

The Gold Rush was worldwide by 1849. London and Paris were headquarters for European crowds clamoring to leave for California. The French conducted many lotteries, and those with lucky tickets won free trips to the gold mines. "The Lottery of the Golden Ingots" was the most popular bargain: only one franc (twenty-four cents) a chance.

Parisians were particularly optimistic. One company brought along furniture and prefabricated houses so that its members could enjoy the comforts of home in the "wild West."[9] Another group planned to build hotels near the mines as a great money-making investment. Collecting gold seemed so simple that some deluded Frenchmen packed rakes to rake in gold "leaves." The expectation of huge profits even intrigued charities. They paid adventurers to dig gold to benefit the poor.[10]

It wasn't only the lure of riches that motivated Europeans to leave for the United States. During 1848 there had been political uprisings in France, the Italian states, Germany, Hungary, and Rumania. Unemployment and food shortages caused terrible suffering. America offered an escape to a land of opportunity. Thousands of people from all over the world migrated, not only to seek their fortunes, but also to find a better way of life.

Lewis Miller drew this sketch of his group, the California Company, which set out from York, Pennsylvania, in 1849.

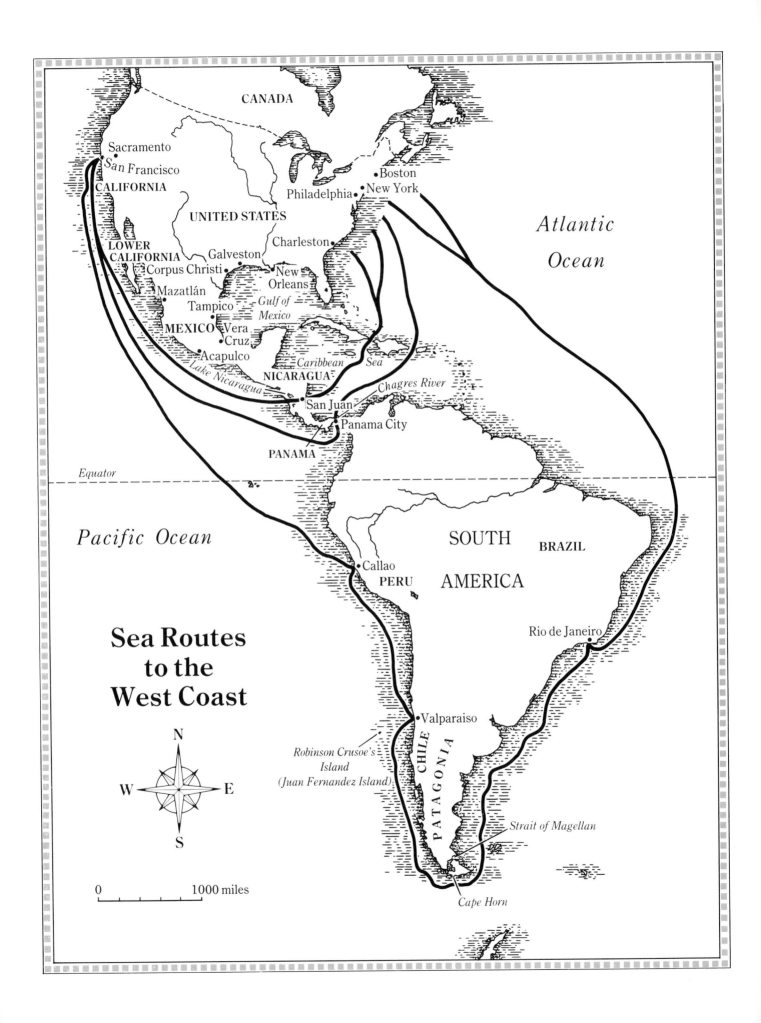

CANADA

Sacramento
San Francisco
CALIFORNIA

UNITED STATES

Boston
Philadelphia New York

Atlantic

Ocean

**LOWER
CALIFORNIA**
Corpus Christi

Charleston

Galveston

New
Orleans

Mazatlán
Tampico

*Gulf of
Mexico*

MEXICO Vera
Cruz

Acapulco

Caribbean Sea

Lake Nicaragua **NICARAGUA**

Chagres River

San Juan
Panama City

PANAMA

Equator

Pacific Ocean

SOUTH

BRAZIL

Callao
PERU

AMERICA

Rio de Janeiro

Sea Routes
to the
West Coast

Valparaiso

N

*Robinson Crusoe's
Island
(Juan Fernandez Island)*

W   E

CHILE

PATAGONIA

S

Strait of Magellan

0   1000 miles

Cape Horn

3 · SHORTCUTS: PANAMA, NICARAGUA, MEXICO

$\mathbf{P}$EOPLE FEARED that if they didn't get to the diggings in a hurry, all the gold would be gone. They had to gather nuggets while they lasted. How awful if after a long journey they arrived too late, when all the gold had already been picked and pocketed.

The Panama Route

The Panama route was unquestionably shortest and swiftest. Travelers might be at the diggings in a matter of weeks! It sounded so easy: Just board a ship bound for an Atlantic port in Panama; cross the isthmus by mule, canoe, or on foot; once on the Pacific side catch a ship that is headed for California.

Ships that advertised space sold out within hours. To insure reservations people often made travel arrangements through shipping agents, who guaranteed safety and comfort. Customers anticipated a lovely cruise in the Atlantic, a week in which to enjoy Panama's tropical splendor, then a delightful Pacific Ocean cruise. After that, gold-gathering!

One passenger took along fifteen buckskin bags that could store three hundred pounds of treasure. Another had a trunk with a false bottom for hiding and protecting his loot.

Gold-seekers booked passage on any old tub that floated. They had a tough time tolerating filth, foul food, and rough seas. But dreams of riches helped them cope with misery.

Those who could afford the finest accommodations took steamships. The most expensive quarters consisted of small cabins with two to four berths—far superior to second class, where twelve to fifteen passengers were shoehorned into one room. Steerage, the cheapest fare, was horrible. People slept on shelves six feet long and eighteen inches wide, stacked one above the other. No room to sit up. They ate lying down or standing in narrow passageways. A New York doctor who visited steerage quarters was shocked at the vile conditions: 160 men in the hold that had only one hatch for ventilation. "Nine men occupied the space of but six feet square," he observed.[1] On overcrowded ships, passengers often paid to sleep in lifeboats.

Some travelers were armed with pistols and knives, ready for battle. They expected to fight savages in Panama. New Yorker John Letts placed two revolvers in his belt, a brace of small pistols inside his coat, and a slingshot in his pocket. He sported a cane that hid a knife. He and his friends stepped off the ship in Panama and "looked for the enemy."[2]

The "enemy" turned out to be poor, harmless natives who lived in the port of Chagres, a squalid village of windowless bamboo huts. When this sleepy Panamanian town was suddenly overrun with gold-seekers, the natives were pleased at the chance to earn money. However, they were upset by the pushiness and superior attitude of the foreigners, who scurried off ships shouting for service. In a panic to get going, travelers vied with each other to hire dugouts, called *bungos*. Natives would paddle and pole these boats westward for seventy-five miles along the Chagres River to Gorgona.

Makeshift sleeping quarters on a crowded ship

After that, a short overland trip would bring passengers to the Pacific port of Panama City.

A typical bungo carried from four to ten passengers. At first the price was ten dollars a passenger, but as crowds crushed into Chagres boatmen raised their rates to forty and fifty dollars. The unexpected expense infuriated many, especially those who had packed trunks filled with clothes and

Traveling by bungo
on the Chagres River

supplies. They had to leave these behind and consider them a total loss, or else pay an additional charge for space on the bungo. Sensible travelers who had overpacked abandoned most of their belongings.

The boat trip took from three to five days. Boatmen saw no reason to hurry. Life was difficult enough. Why race and make work harder than ever? Many passengers were exasperated. In their prejudiced opinion all natives were stupid, lazy good-for-nothings.

The boatmen were shocked by the rudeness and roughness of some travelers. In at least one case, California-bound ruffians threatened to blow out the brains of boatmen who didn't paddle fast enough to suit them.

The first stop after Chagres was Gatun, where passengers paid for a night's shelter in flea-infested huts. Some slept on the floor; others rented hammocks. Passengers griped about the heat, humidity, and rain squalls. Some, fearing insects, scorpions, snakes, and alligators, chose to bed down in the boats. Others, delighted by the jungle's flowers and birds, enjoyed stopovers.

The boat trip ended at Gorgona, but if heavy rains kept the river deep, travelers continued another four miles to Cruces. Once again, everyone haggled for transportation. Mules, horses, or porters were needed for a rugged twenty-mile overland trip. Although some found the jungle exciting because of its spectacular scenery and exotic wildlife—including monkeys, parrots, anteaters, and anacondas—others detested the crossing. Mules and horses were often bogged down in mud. The narrow trail across the jungle and over the mountains was rough. Oppressive heat and swarming insects were aggravating, and many travelers became seriously ill.

Rough riding across Panama

From 1848 to 1854 cholera was rampant in various parts of North America. This dread disease can kill within hours. Persons who feel fine in the morning can be dead by afternoon. It spreads quickly. During 1849, it raged in Panama.[3] Yellow fever, also called "Panama fever," was another killer. In addition, dysentery and typhoid took their toll. The causes of these illnesses weren't known at that time. The journey across the Panamanian jungle claimed the lives of countless gold-seekers. Despite this, the isthmus way remained a popular route for years.[4]

Although most of the forty-niners were men, women also headed for the mines. Bayard Taylor, a newspaperman covering the Gold Rush for the New York *Herald,* saw a woman from Maine fording a stream, aided by two natives, who held on to her so that the waist-high torrential waters wouldn't carry her away. He also wrote about a French lady who was "washed from her mule, and only got over by the united exertions of seven men." Taylor saw unchaperoned women who crossed the isthmus wearing men's clothes— shocking at that time, but a corsetless, comfortable way to dress.[5]

As a result of the Gold Rush stampede, Panama City on the Pacific coast developed into a busy port with hotels, bars, and gambling houses geared for Americans. Although this city was supposed to be a hasty stopover before boarding a ship to California, thousands of travelers were trapped. They had to wait for months because space on ocean vessels was oversold. Whenever a ticket became available, it was bought immediately for as much as one thousand dollars. Most travelers were stranded, marooned in a place they hated, forced to wait for a ship that could take them aboard.

Several small groups became so stir-crazy that they bought canoes and tried to paddle up the Pacific to San Francisco. After weeks at sea, nearly all of them returned to

Panama City, happy to have survived an ordeal. Those who didn't return were never heard from again.

The 1849 cholera epidemic raged in Panama City. According to Bayard Taylor, the disease killed one-fourth of the native population and took a heavy toll among American gold-seekers.[6] Instead of waiting for their ship to come in, some of the frightened, horrified travelers turned back and headed for home.

Passage to San Francisco

Gold-seekers waiting in Panama City were anxious for the arrival of the steamship *California.* The *California,* one of the United States's newest mail carriers, was equipped with rooms for passengers. It had left New York harbor in October 1848, before the East's Gold Rush excitement. When it docked at Callao, Peru, in December, South Americans had already learned about the discovery of gold in California. Seventy Peruvian gold-seekers bought space aboard.

Crossing the isthmus

When the *California* docked in Panama City on January 17, 1849, crowds were in an uproar. Stranded Americans were furious that foreigners occupied berths on a United States ship. They demanded that the ship's captain oust the Peruvians and make room for "real Americans." Captain Marshall refused to do so, but mollified mobs by ordering the Peruvians to move out of staterooms and camp on deck.[7]

United States citizens took over first-class staterooms and crowded on to every part of the ship. When the *California* left Panama City, 365 passengers were aboard, although there was officially room for no more than 250. As a result, the ship ran out of food and fuel. To complete the voyage the captain ripped out berths and even took away parts of the deck in order to feed wood into the ship's boilers.

Everyone was in such a frenzy to reach the mines when the *California* arrived in San Francisco on February 28th that the entire crew deserted. The captain of the next steamship to reach San Francisco from Panama anchored his ship, the *Oregon,* close to a United States man-of-war, and he put shackles on crewmen so that they couldn't desert. Despite this, some escaped and got to shore using the ship's dinghy.

Sailing ships, whalers, coal ships, fishing boats—anything that floated—accepted paying customers from Panama City to San Francisco. The starvation diet, rationed water, and filth were so unbearable that many got off the boats in Mexico and lower California. They journeyed overland on foot or horseback rather than endure more sea travel.

The Nicaragua Route

After letters and newspapers told about conditions in Panama, many gold-seekers decided to cross the continent by way of Nicaragua. Nicaragua, five hundred miles north of Panama, is closer to the United States. Although its landmass is wider than Panama's, the trip was thought to be quicker and easier.

A promoter named George Gordon (who called himself a "practical geologist") printed alluring circulars that guaranteed a comfortable and healthful shortcut to California: across Nicaragua by way of the San Juan River and Lake Nicaragua, then sixty miles on "a well travelled road" to the Pacific. Gordon assured patrons that they would arrive at the California mines in "50 to 60 days." If it took longer, each passenger would receive a seventy-five dollar refund, plus sixty days' worth of provisions. In March 1849, Gordon's enterprise, the California Association, left New York harbor on a chartered ship, the *Mary*. It was filled to capacity with 136 enthusiastic passengers.

When the *Mary* docked at San Juan, Nicaragua, it unloaded the steamboat *Plutus,* which had been brought along in parts. This steamboat was supposed to take passengers upriver and across Lake Nicaragua. However, after the *Plutus* was assembled, it was obvious that the boat wasn't safe. Everyone had to travel by bungo, Panama-style. Six weeks in native canoes; then another long wait before arrangements were made to proceed on muleback. (And they were supposed to be on a well-traveled road, suitable for stagecoaches!) When they finally reached a Pacific port, there was no ship waiting for them, even though they had paid in advance for accommodations. Gordon's clients were castaways stranded on the coast of Nicaragua.

Waiting for a ship at Panama City

Stranded in Panama City

They waited three months, until Gordon chartered a ship. Then, instead of receiving the promised refund, each passenger had to pay more money in order to proceed.

Although the trip was supposed to take fifty or sixty days, it took eight months. Some of Gordon's customers, who couldn't afford to board a ship, took a bungo into the ocean and were never heard from again. Others rented a small sailboat that was becalmed in one spot for so long that they nearly starved to death.

At sea, Gordon's clients learned that drinking water was rationed and the food was revolting. One of them wrote that "the bread was full of worms and defiled with cockroaches; the rice was half hulls, with as many weevils as kernels."[8]

The Nicaragua route, which had been touted as a grand holiday venture, was a terrible fiasco.[9]

The Mexico Route

Since Panama and Nicaragua had their drawbacks, some gold-seekers crossed Mexico to get to the Pacific. People boarded ships at New Orleans, Galveston, Corpus Christi, and other gulf ports. It was a short voyage for them and seemed the logical route to take. Ships also left from New York and Philadelphia for Mexico.

First, Tampico or Vera Cruz on Mexico's east coast. After that, a terrible trek over mountains and deserts to the Pacific coast to find a California-bound ship. Popular guidebooks had assured travelers that there was no need for concern. Maps showed smooth roads that didn't exist and neglected to indicate deserts and mountains.

Cholera felled so many passengers on ships that burials at sea were commonplace. In Mexico travelers were horrified by the prevalence of the plague. After passing through villages of the dying, many gold-seekers gave up their quest for treasure and returned to their homes in the United States.

Those who kept going reached Acapulco, Mazatlan, or San Blas on the Pacific coast. But they were no better off than those who took the Panama and Nicaragua routes. Travelers boarded miserable crafts with rotting food and rationed drinking water. Any kind of boat found paying customers.

The run from Mexico to California was so profitable that the king of Hawaii sent a condemned whaler across the Pacific. His boat had "... no fixtures save the bare, oil soaked decks, old oil barrels for water tanks, and as a cooking range two try kettles in a furnace."[10] Each person was allotted space measuring four feet by eight feet.

At least the king's whaler made it to San Francisco, whereas many other vessels sank or broke down and had to head for shore. Daniel Woods, a Philadelphia schoolteacher, was so terrified by the rough voyage that he and several others asked to be put ashore along the Mexican coast. They trudged through deserts and climbed jagged mountains in order to find drinking water. The group zigzagged fifteen hundred miles, surviving on cactus fruit and leaves. After reaching San Diego, they were lucky to find a ship to San Francisco.

A company called the New England Pioneers expected to cross Mexico on horseback in twenty-nine days and spend another month on a ship to San Francisco. However, only four horses were available at Vera Cruz, and therefore most of them had to walk across Mexico. When they reached the west coast port of San Blas, there was no space available on any ship. They finally chartered their own schooner, which they abandoned at lower California after a hair-raising, unsafe voyage, then trudged north to the diggings.

4 · THE CAPE HORN ROUTE

FOR EASTERNERS living near the Atlantic Ocean, a sea voyage to the other side of America seemed the best and easiest way to go. Why risk the hardships and health hazards of land travel in Panama, Mexico, or Nicaragua when there was an all-water route? Plenty of ships kept leaving New York and New England ports for California by looping around Cape Horn. Although the journey would be long, passengers visualized an enjoyable, clean, comfortable cruise. Booking passage on a ship manned by experienced sailors sounded safe and sensible. Easterners enthusiastically embarked on a fifteen thousand-mile sea voyage that took at least six months—and sometimes lasted a year.[1]

Advertisements promised luxury accommodations and carefree hours of pleasure. High-priced tickets on ocean-going ships sold out quickly. Whaling skippers gladly used their boats for paying customers, jamming them into quarters usually reserved for blubber and whale oil. Merchant ships crowded their holds with passengers who slept in space usually allotted for cargo.

More than five hundred ships crammed with customers set out from Atlantic and gulf ports during 1849. The Cape Horn route was also popular with European gold-seekers

A PASSAGE TO THE GOLD REGION FOR $75 !

FOR SAN FRANCISCO DIRECT.

THE SPLENDID A. No. 1 NEWLY COPPERED

PACKET SHIP APOLLO.

recently in the European trade, having most of her freight engaged, will sail for

SAN FRANCISCO, CALIFORNIA,

and the gold region in that vicinity, from the

Foot of Chambers Street, North River,

WHERE SHE NOW LIES, ON THE SECOND OF JANUARY NEXT.

Passengers will be taken on the following terms;

Steerage Passage - - - - - - - $ 75.
Cabin Passage - - - - - - - - - 150.
Ditto out and home - - - - - - 200·
Ditto with board while there 250.

Several Families can be Accommodated.

The advantages offered to passengers by this conveyance cannot be surpassed. The APOLLO is one of the safest and most airy ships in New York, and has few equals in speed. She is destined to sail *directly*, not only for San Francisco, but, if it can be done as is expected, she is to be taken up the Sacramento river thirty or forty miles, into the very heart of the Gold Region, where she is to remain for some time.

The voyage each way, it is expected will be made in about four months.

Persons intending to take passage by this vessel will do well to secure their berths *at the earliest possible moment*, as the ship will, in a day or two be occupied entirely by Carpenters, Stevedores and other Mechanics, busily engaged in fitting up berths, stowing freight, taking in a supply of provisions, and making other preparations for the voyage. Choice of Berths will be given to passengers in the order of the numbers upon their passage tickets.

Freight taken on consignment or otherwise, at the lowest rates.

No Passage secured until paid for.

who set sail from England and France. Thousands of passengers joined companies, so that their enterprise would be a group effort. There were also men and women who booked single passage. Newspapers called California-bound travelers "argonauts" after the gold-seeking heros of ancient Greek mythology.

Before departure, there were often elaborate farewell ceremonies with hymns, prayers, and sermons. President Edward Everett of Harvard preached to a company of 150 Boston gold-getters about leaving civilization. "You are going to a strange country," he warned. "Take the Bible in one hand and your New England civilization in the other and make your mark on the people and the country."[2] They had a mission: to spread culture in the primitive, wild West—and to bring back native California gold. As a going-away gift, Everett donated a library of one hundred books (that probably included the essays of Ralph Waldo Emerson and the poetry of Henry Wadsworth Longfellow and John Greenleaf Whittier).

Passengers on the *Sweden* received a different type of present: a white satin banner. It depicted men leaving the ship and climbing a hill of gold. A speaker urged his listeners to carry the banner when they ascended to new heights of wealth.

Expectations were so high that a man who embarked from New York tossed a five-dollar gold piece to the dockside crowd. "I'm going where there is plenty more," he shouted.[3] Members of a Hartford company were also unrealistic. According to their rules, after they reached the diggings each member was expected to make daily deposits of gold in the company's safe. If the gold was so heavy that it overloaded the ship, piles of the precious metal could be left on shore—under guard, of course. Arrangements would be made to ship the excess heaps later.

Many companies planned to add to their profits by selling

merchandise to Californians. A new, expanding market had opened up because of the West's population explosion. Odd items were stocked in ships' holds: ladies' bonnets and dresses (although there were few women miners in '49); fur-lined overcoats (not suitable for mild California winters); and swords (possibly for fashion rather than fighting). There were also crystal chandeliers (for future mansions), pianos (for recitals), French wines (for gracious living), and on a more practical side, prefabricated houses, lumber, nails, needles, shovels, and wheelbarrows.

Few knew what to expect. As a result, many set off with huge strongboxes for hoarding gold dust, small cannons for fighting Indians, cumbersome machines for mining, and trunks filled with fancy party clothes.

Once the ships were launched, reality hit in strong waves. Never in their wildest dreams had landlubbers imagined a churning sea that would knock them around and make them sick to their stomachs. When the ocean became calm, it could be relaxing but very boring. Reading, keeping journals,

Argonaut Isaac Baker sketched this shipboard scene.

This fanciful sketch
is from Baker's journal
entry for October 28, 1849.

gambling, and card playing took away some of the tedium. Bostonians aboard the *Everett* battled monotony with intellectual shipboard activities. There were Shakespearean recitations, lectures on scientific subjects, and a weekly newspaper, called the *Barometer,* which published passengers' prose and poetry. Prayer meetings and sermons were also scheduled.

Drinking hard liquor made time pass. However, many companies forbade drinking. Quite a few men signed oaths pledging never to drink anything containing alcohol. Some groups had "Rules of Behavior" that forbade card playing and cursing. Punishments took the form of fines or doing time cleaning up the ship.

Life aboard ship could be miserable. Jam-packed in cabins and below-deck bunks, passengers were stifled by foul air. No room to move. They roasted in tropical seas and froze in Antarctic waters. A trip they had anticipated as an adventure turned out to be a grim ordeal.

As a rule, the food was awful. After weeks at sea, fresh produce rotted and had to be thrown overboard. In days before refrigeration, the usual shipboard menu consisted of salt meat or fish, potatoes, beans, and hardtack. "Two bugs for every bean," one diarist remarked. "Coffee bad, sugar dirty, and bread wormy," another wrote.[4]

The lack of fruit and vegetables resulted in scurvy, a sickness caused by the lack of vitamin C. People wasted away, lost their hair and teeth, and if the disease persisted for a long time, they died. The cure could be immediate. Potatoes, cabbage, even pickles, dried fruit, or jams could stop the disease, and, better still, prevent it. On one ship a crafty fellow sold prunes to others at one dollar apiece. On another, a passenger kept his own box of preserved quinces to himself. "I often take a spoonful on the sly," he wrote.[5]

Drinking water was another problem. Stored in wooden casks, it became stagnant and stinking. "The water is becoming *bad*," a passenger wrote. ". . . I don't mind it much. I have a way of killing the bugs before drinking them."[6]

Although most people griped about meals, some were so riled they considered mutiny. They restrained themselves, however, because they could submit their grievances to an American consul if the ship stopped at Rio de Janeiro. A consul had the authority to remove incompetent captains, levy fines against ship owners, and arrest mutinous crews. Passengers on one of the runs of the *Pacific,* for example, informed the consul about the awful meals they were served. They defied Captain Tibbets, who had posted a notice threatening to clamp complainers in irons. Although there was good food on board, the captain never served it. He expected to pocket profits by selling the food in San Francisco. The consul dismissed Tibbets and replaced him with a new skipper, Captain Estherbrook.

Rio was a large city whose residents were accustomed to "emigrant Californians" touring their beautiful buildings and using their hotels and bars. Slave markets horrified visitors, especially those from New England. Unlike Southern slaveholders, they had never witnessed humans for sale. "Here were offered strong men, robust women and children, for sale the same as donkeys and goats," one voyager reported.[7] The stopover usually lasted just a few days, until the ship could take on fresh supplies. Although most captains were honorable, several crooked skippers deliberately sailed away without their passengers. They profited by saving money on food and by selling the empty places to new passengers at another port. It meant full fare a second time.

Rounding the Cape

Terrifying seas battered ships at Cape Horn. Rounding it could take weeks. There were days when wind and waves pushed vessels far off course, and people begged the captain to turn back. The ocean was so rough that passengers lashed down belongings and tied themselves to their berths to keep from being tossed around and slammed about. Life below deck was agony, but anyone on deck risked being swept overboard by mammoth waves.

Instead of rounding Cape Horn, some captains sailed through the Strait of Magellan. It cut hundreds of miles from the journey, but this storm-lashed three hundred–mile passage had treacherous currents. In some places it was so narrow that getting through required skill—and luck. One sorry ship took two and a half months to reach the Pacific. It was scary, especially when passengers saw the floating wreckage of other ships.

Another frightening prospect was being shipwrecked on the shores of Patagonia, then rumored to be a land of cannibals and dog-headed monsters. The one safe anchorage along the strait was Port Famine, a former convicts' colony, described as "the most horrible and gloomy place you can imagine."[8] Ships stopped there to wait out storms.

Once the Pacific was reached, a gold-seeker's journey could prove to be a pleasure: calm seas and the hopes of a prosperous voyage. Sometimes men went boating, fishing, and swimming. Whale- and dolphin-watching were common pastimes. Capturing albatrosses was another. Using fish as bait, passengers on the *Orion* caught these giant birds and measured them: more than twelve feet, wing to wing.

It was customary to stop at either Valparaiso, Chile, or Callao, Peru, in order to replenish ship supplies. The seaports gave gold-seekers relief from shipboard life and a chance to visit a foreign country.

Robinson Crusoe's Island (Juan Fernandez Island) was another tourist's delight. While the ship dropped anchor so that the crew could collect wood, fresh water, and fruit, passengers took excursions to a cave supposedly occupied by Crusoe. (It didn't seem to matter that the story about a shipwrecked Englishman was fiction.) Some stayed overnight, hosted by a few people who lived on the island. They were treated to tourist accommodations Crusoe-style: a goatskin on the floor for a bed; a crude shack for a hotel. Travelers declared that Crusoe was lucky, because the island had plenty of fresh water and lots of peach, quince, apple, and fig trees.

Returning to ship from Crusoe's Island was a pleasure because there would be better meals, and the roughest part of the journey was behind them.[9]

There was an almost hysterical amount of activity the week before landing in San Francisco. After spending monotonous months doing little, gold-seekers started getting ready for California. They cleaned guns, polished pistols, and sharpened tools. They looked over their machines for minting coins and gadgets for digging gold. They cut canvases for tents and repaired clothes. Everyone was about to enter the promised land.

5 · OVERLAND

WHILE PEOPLE IN THE EAST clamored to board ships bound for California, those in the Midwest prepared to go overland. For them the direct way to the gold fields lay straight across the plains, and they streamed west by the thousands. Traveling overland also attracted Easterners who preferred land to sea travel. Most gold-seekers chose overland routes.[1] The main attraction of land travel was financial. No need for expensive tickets on ships. Farmers hitched oxen or mules to the family wagon, stocked up on food, and headed west. Companies usually purchased their animals and wagons when they reached a Missouri river town.

St. Joseph, Independence, Council Bluffs, and other frontier towns were jump-off points to start the main trail to California. Businesses boomed as traders sold everything from axes to oxen. Gambling houses and drinking saloons became hangouts to squander cash and while away time. Hotels were so jam-packed that two or three men were often assigned to the same bed.

Everybody was anxious to set out on a two thousand-mile journey that might take five months. Because there had to be enough spring grass on the prairies to feed their animals, no one with any sense dared to depart before April or May. And it was foolhardy to start after June because snow might

Buying supplies in a river town

block mountain passes by the time they reached the Sierras.[2]

Companies usually had their camps out of town, because it was cheaper. Twenty-year-old William Johnson from Pittsburgh was naive enough to believe that by sleeping in tents his group would learn about the "hardships such as one might encounter on the plains."[3]

Overland routes to the West had been pioneered by fur traders and mapped out by military explorers before 1849. The trails had been especially helpful for settlers bound for Oregon and for the few pioneers headed for California. Unfortunately, even the most reliable maps didn't indicate where there would be barren land, parching heat, and bone-chilling cold.

Many city people had never handled mules or oxen, couldn't fix wagons, and didn't know how to hunt. They were going to ford rivers, climb mountains, and stumble through deserts. They didn't anticipate violent storms, bruising hailstones, prairie fires, rattlesnakes, grizzly bears, spoiled food, and broken-down wagons. Those who failed to join companies with experienced outdoorsmen ran the greatest risk of being stranded or lost in the wilderness.

Nevertheless, many preferred to be on their own. Some used ox-drawn wagons, others rode horses or mules. A few lone adventurers walked across North America. A Scotsman from Pennsylvania pushed his wheelbarrow over plains and mountains, and a man from Michigan walked lugging a large box under his arm containing one treasured possession, his violin.[4]

Typical emigrants were armed with guns and knives to protect themselves from so-called "wild Indians." Overland companies were usually organized like military units. Officers issued commands, conducted infantry drills, posted guards, and decided when to camp and what direction to take. Their wagons were stocked with pistols, rifles, knives, and swords. A Massachusetts group mounted swivel guns on each wagon. An Iowa company insisted that each man carry thirty pounds of lead for making bullets. Wagons and livestock were guarded by "walking arsenals." According to an Illinois traveler, "The multitude of armed men looked as if a mighty army was on the march."[5]

A crowded mountain pass

Sioux Indians

There were instances of Indians stealing livestock, but in general, Indians did not confront emigrants. Tribesmen frequently visited them to trade for food and guns. Some travelers scorned them as dirty, naked, untrustworthy beggars; others decided they were "noble savages."[6]

While armed for imagined battles against Indians, emigrants were not able to ward off the real enemy—cholera. The disease hit Missouri in April 1849, just when crowds had congregated to head west. Cholera traveled and disembarked from riverboats. (One steamship that left St. Louis for St. Joseph became a "death ship" when within one week, seventy of its one hundred cabin passengers died from the disease.) The disease ravaged the river towns. In a letter to his relatives in Missouri, D. Moss wrote, "We lost two of our company of 17, one of them . . . taken down with cholera about 75 miles from the Mo. river, and died in seven hours after first complaining."[7] Panicky emigrants pushed to get going, believing they could escape illness. They not only had to race for riches, but also to speed away from a plague. Some gulped gunpowder as a medicine; others either drank liquor as a preventative or gave it up, believing that drink caused the disease.

In their haste to get going, emigrants lined up their wagons for miles at Missouri River ferry crossings. At St. Joseph, where hundreds waited day and night for their turn, two wagon drivers shot and killed each other after arguing over their place in line. During April, the wait took weeks; by May the estimated delay was two months.

J. Goldsborough Bruff, a government draftsman who headed the Washington City Company of sixty-six men, led his group north of St. Joseph looking for a less crowded ferry crossing. At one place he watched a raft capsize and sink:

"Mr. Duncan, the worthy proprietor of the Ferry,—steering the boat, was most unfortunately drowned."[8] Bruff's group continued along the shores of the Platte River until the men found a safe ferry.

Bruff's group was lucky. Deaths by drowning were commonplace at stream and river crossings. An Ohio diarist who was appalled at the number of drownings described a ferry crossing as "a little like a battlefield."[9]

"Crossing of the Platte Mouth of Deer Creek,"
by Franklin R. Grist

OREGON
TERRITORY

UNORGANIZED
TERRITORY

MINNESOTA
TERRITORY

Rocky

*Black Rock
Desert*

*Independence
Rock*

Laramie R.

Missouri

P l a i n s

*South
Pass*

North

*Humboldt
Sink*

*Humboldt
River*

Sweetwater R.

River

Sacramento R.

■ Fort Laramie

Forty Mile Desert

■ Salt Lake City

Platte R.

Platte R.

*American
R.*

Sutter's Fort (Sacramento)•
•Sutter's Mill

UTAH TERRITORY

Chimney Rock

■ Fort
Kearney

San Francisco•

Sierra

• Monterey

Nevada

Colorado R.

M

o

*Death
Valley*

u

CALIFORNIA

NEW MEXICO
TERRITORY

•Santa Fe

n

Pacific

•Los Angeles

t

Ocean

•San Diego

*Colorado
Desert*

Gila R.

a

TEXAS

i

Guadalupe

n

N

Sierra Madre

Mts.

s

W   E

•Chihuahua

Rio Grande

S

M E X I C O

Corpus Christi•

Monterrey•

The most frequently used overland trail followed the Platte River to Fort Kearney and on to Fort Laramie, then crossed the South Pass of the Rockies. Many argonauts then followed the Humboldt River to the Humboldt Sink and went through the Forty Mile Desert to the Sierra Nevada diggings.

An inexperienced buffalo hunter

Fort Kearney on the Platte River was a usual stopover. Traffic became incredibly heavy. A newspaper correspondent counted 180 wagons coming by on a single day: one every five minutes. Before continuing four hundred miles along the Platte River, emigrants stopped at the fort to post letters, buy supplies, visit the fort's doctors, and ply officers with questions about trails.

Buffalo herds were a common sight on the plains. Men looked forward to hunting buffalo, not only because of the meat—the tongue and hump were especially tasty—but also for the sport. It was dangerous! Wounded bulls charged and injured hunters. Many were seriously hurt. Despite this, bored, bold gold-seekers took their chances. They played a role in the wanton destruction of buffalo. In one case, fifty buffalo were killed—although only three were used for meat.[10]

The trail along the Platte River was fairly easy, on flat, wide-open country.[11] There were times along the way when a company seemed to have the prairie all to itself. At other times, thousands of slow-moving wagons crowded the trails as far as the eye could see. A great migration was taking place. It disrupted families and left many communities short of able-bodied young men.

Overburdened draft animals went lame and collapsed from exhaustion. Hoping to ease the pain, some emigrants made leather moccasins for oxen feet. They soon realized

THE GREAT AMERICAN GOLD RUSH

that they were lugging too many useless articles, and that by unloading, they might save their livestock. Clothing, rocking chairs, blacksmith's tools, mining machines, iron stoves, pickaxes, and shovels were thrown away to make loads lighter. Hundreds of wagons were left along the wayside when the animals that pulled them sickened or died.

Even food was discarded. Piles of bacon, bags of sugar, and sacks of flour were dumped because they were too heavy to carry. Notes were often left urging others to take the food, assuring them that even though thrown away, it was good. But mean characters deliberately spoiled food. They poured turpentine on sugar, mixed flour with dirt, tore discarded clothes, and broke abandoned wagons, "simply because the owners could not use it themselves and were determined that nobody else should."[12]

J. Goldsborough Bruff drew this, and hundreds of other sketches, while traveling overland to California.

Most appalling were the numerous graves along the trails, mainly of cholera victims. Usually, the dead were buried with wooden markers planted over their graves. Indian tribes were decimated by the disease, carried west by the emigrants. Sioux, Pawnee, and Cheyenne tribes were especially affected. Emigrants reported entering tents and lodges only to find dead Indians inside.

Overlanders usually camped near Fort Laramie, an important military post at the junction of the North Platte and Laramie rivers. It had been used by fur traders until the government purchased it from them in 1849 for the sum of four thousand dollars. At Laramie, travelers could have their wagons repaired, engage a blacksmith, and buy groceries and other supplies. Like Fort Kearney, it acted as a post office, where emigrants picked up letters from home and sent back

Fort Laramie

THE GREAT AMERICAN GOLD RUSH

Hailstorm in the Platte
Valley, sketched by Bruff

notes to concerned friends, lonely wives, and worried parents. William Swain was disheartened when he realized that a long letter he had written to his wife would take at least three months to be delivered to her in Youngstown, New York.

The worst hardships took place after leaving Laramie. Grass was sparse and animals died of starvation. There were days without decent water, only mud puddles by the roadside "or green slimy water standing at the bottom of some ravines."[13] They drank it to survive, often holding their noses so that the stench wouldn't sicken them. Along many stretches the water was poisonous. After drinking it, people became violently ill, and animals died. A considerate traveler posted this notice: "Look at this—look at this! The water here is poison and we have lost six of our cattle. Do not let your cattle drink on this bottom."[14] Keeping thirsty livestock away from the water was often impossible.

Emigrants were bewildered by a landscape they had never envisioned. Violent storms were terrifying. Hundreds of animals went berserk and ran off during fierce rain squalls. People spent days searching in vain for their oxen, horses, and mules. Men, women, and children wandered about, dazed, distracted, and helpless.

Hailstorms were brutal. During one, "the air was literally

filled with balls of ice from the size of a walnut to that of a *goose egg.*" As a result there were "gashed heads, black eyes, pounded and swollen backs, shoulders and arms . . . The cattle were many of them cut through on the hips and back by hail."[15] At least one group found a use for the heaven-sent ice. The Marietta Gold Hunters of Ohio used it to chill brandy.

Crossing the deep, swift-flowing North Platte River was an obstacle that caused aggravating delays. Enterprising Mormons from Salt Lake City had set up a ferry service. Groups queued up to be floated across at three dollars per wagon; fifty cents per person. Here, as along the Missouri, traffic jams were so frustrating that many companies used

Eight canoes were lashed together to make this raft.

nearby cottonwood trees to build their own ferries. Some travelers caulked the cracks, removed the wheels, and floated their wagons across, using ropes to steady them. Teamsters drowned trying to force their animals to swim rivers. There were other casualties when makeshift rafts capsized.

Beyond the crossings of the North Platte the country changed. It was stark, barren land containing pools of poisonous water. The argonauts trudged through this desert, passing putrid carcasses of livestock. Dead animals littered the landscape, and because there were few trees and no buffalo chips (manure) for making fires, emigrants often chopped up wagons and used the wood for fuel.

It was a relief to arrive at the Sweetwater River, appreciated because of its pure waters. After that, emigrants went on the South Pass of the Rockies. It was a wide slope that rose so gradually that emigrants never knew the moment they crossed the Continental Divide—a height in the Rocky Mountains that separates the eastward-flowing streams from the westward-flowing waters. Because of the high elevation, people suffered from the cold.[16]

After the South Pass, trails branched in different directions. Travelers had to descend the western slopes of the Rockies, then zigzag through valleys and canyons for hundreds of miles.

Some argonauts looked forward to the Humboldt River, described in one guidebook as "rich and beautifully clothed in blue grass, herds grass, clover and other nutritious grasses," offering everything "for the emigrants' comfort, in abundance."[17] In reality, grass was in such short supply that travelers foraged for it and carried it to their livestock. Alkaline dust irritated their throats and eyes, and the air stank from animal carcasses.

The long pull along the Humboldt River was also distressing because emigrants were uncomfortable among the native Indians. Scorned as the "Diggers" because they sub-

The wagons of the Washington City and California Gold Mining Association are drawn into a circle for defense against Indians. Note the names of the forty-niners carved into Independence Rock (in the foreground).

THE GREAT AMERICAN GOLD RUSH

sisted upon roots and insects, these Indians were despised by the emigrants because they occasionally stole animals and ate them in order to relieve their near-starvation diet. "Trappers and travellers shoot them down without hesitation or remorse wherever they meet them," a British gold-seeker noted.[18]

After 365 miles, the Humboldt disappeared into a marshy bog called the Sink, "an ocean of ooze, a bottomless bed of alkaline poison which emitted a nauseous odor and presented the appearance of utter desolation."[19] Beyond this stretched the dreaded Forty Mile Desert, where nothing grew. It stretched from the Sink to the foot of the Sierra Nevada. The sole water supply consisted of springs and geysers that spouted boiling hot, stinking water. Heat, exhaustion, parched throats, and swollen tongues made pushing forward an ordeal.

After the desert, trails twisted and turned through steep canyons. At times people had to lift wagons to get them around bends. The Buckeye Rovers of Ohio "let the wagons down the rocks some sixty feet in one place, and in other places . . . kept the cattle on but attached ropes to ease wagons down."[20] Giant boulders broke wagon wheels, and a seemingly endless succession of ice-cold streams had to be forded before reaching the Sierra Nevada. By the time emigrants climbed mountains, many were starving, and many suffered from scurvy, that awful disease caused by the lack of fruits and vegetables.

Alternate Routes

To avoid the Humboldt Sink, many emigrants tried what they hoped would be a better route. After crossing the Rockies, they headed for Salt Lake City, the Mormon capital that was founded in 1847. It was a pleasant town where emigrants relaxed, stocked up on supplies, and bought sound oxen and pack animals. They rested in a city they viewed as an oasis of civilization. Some stayed a few days; others remained for months, waiting for good weather. From Salt Lake City there were several trails to California. The most ghastly choice was one that crossed a desert now known as Death Valley—a name given to it after at least five forty-niners died there from thirst and starvation.[21]

Lassen's route was touted as a shortcut that avoided the Forty Mile Desert. But it added two hundred miles and weeks of exhausting travel to the trek by swinging north toward Oregon before turning south to California. Lassen's "shortcut" was the brainchild of Peter Lassen, who owned a ranch near Oregon where emigrants could buy supplies from him. Captain Bruff and his Washington City Company chose this route. His group trudged through the Black Rock Desert, a forbidding wasteland where mirages confused them. They had visions of blue lakes bordered by lush shade trees. Even oxen were deluded and stampeded toward the mirage, hoping to quench their burning thirst, "and left their swelled-up carcasses over the plain in that direction."[22]

When stories about starvation and suffering reached United States officials in California, relief parties were sent out on rescue missions with food, water, blankets, and transportation for those too sick to travel on their own. One relief party came across customers of the Grand Pioneer Line, a passenger service advertised as being so well organized that clients would ride in comfortable carriages from Missouri and get to California in sixty days. The group was "in quite a crippled condition, having lost thirty of their best mules the night before, by the Indians, and having been on short allowance for several weeks."[23]

Private and government relief parties also rescued the sick and the starving who were trapped in mountains of the

Crossing the Rockies

A log bridge collapses.

Sierra Nevada range. The climb was excruciating for people weakened by hardship and illnesses. Alonzo Delano of Illinois concluded: "Any man who makes a trip by land to California deserves to find a fortune."[24]

Southern Routes

Although most overlanders chose midwest trails, southern routes also drew emigrants. Southern trails were used by comparatively few, probably less than nine thousand. Tens of thousands took the midwest overland trail.[25]

Leaving from Arkansas, Louisiana, or Texas seemed promising because the climate was mild, and anyone in a hurry could set out immediately. Newspapers made it sound so easy. The Corpus Christi *Star* described a path to California that "passes through no wilderness—all thickly settled country."[26] The Arkansas *State Democrat* promised a fine trip "through a country among whose hills is heard . . . the joyous laugh of spring, and whose valley wears the warm smile of eternal summer."[27] No mention was made of steep mountains and the appalling Colorado Desert, where travelers could die of thirst.

There were routes from Texas across northern Mexico through Monterrey and Chihuahua, crossing territory frequented by Comanches and Apaches. In some Mexican towns, bounties were offered for captured Indians and for Indian scalps—"$250 for each live squaw and for each child of either sex under fourteen, $200 for the scalp of a warrior

Mealtime

fourteen or above, and $250 for each live warrior."[28] A member of an Ohio company wrote that some friends received three hundred dollars per scalp—a grisly note about a few who were not typical emigrants. Although travelers feared Indians, only a few hunted to kill them. There is no record that Comanches and Apaches molested travelers during the Gold Rush migration.

Many routes crossing the south converged at Santa Fe, the hub for traders and travelers. A commonly used trail then followed the Rio Grande south for several hundred miles before heading west. The Guadalupe Mountains, the Gila and Colorado rivers, and the Colorado Desert had to be crossed before reaching San Diego or Los Angeles. Once they reached California, argonauts had to make additional arrangements to get to gold country, which was hundreds of miles away.

Southern routes were touted everywhere. A swindler named Parker French shipped 189 people from New York to Texas. He guaranteed a quick overland journey, promising to refund five dollars a day per person if the trip to the gold fields took more than sixty days. After sailing to Texas, French's customers were stranded. They had been promised first-class carriage rides cross-country, over nonexistent roads! A warrant was issued for French's arrest, but he was never caught.[29]

Some gold-seekers died of thirst in deserts; others starved when they lost their way in mountains. But a surprising number arrived in California in excellent condition, ready to start digging at once.

6 · LAND OF PROMISE

SWARMS OF OVERLAND TRAVELERS headed for Sutter's property, where gold had first been found. Marshall, the carpenter who discovered gold, had tacked notices along the American River claiming the land for himself, but people ignored his signs.

Newcomers didn't even respect Sutter's property. They trampled his fields, dug up his grounds, and camped on his land. Sutter was horrified as he witnessed this free-for-all invasion. Sutter's twenty-two-year-old son, August, who hadn't seen his father since he was eight years old, emigrated

from Switzerland in 1848 to work for him. He was shocked at the situation. "Everything belonging to my father was at everybody's disposal," he remarked.[1] August tried to salvage whatever he could by selling lots in New Helvetia. Buyers became the founders of present-day Sacramento.

San Francisco was the chief port for argonauts who came by sea. Because there were no docks, ships dropped anchor offshore in the wide harbor. Hundreds of ships were so close to one another that it took a skilled captain to steer without crashing into another vessel.

Small boats usually surrounded newly arrived ships. Some, acting as ferries, were quickly filled with customers willing to pay any price to reach shore. Others were occupied by businessmen eager to exchange bags of gold for imported products they could sell for profit. There were also San Franciscans who rowed out hoping to find servants. In one case, competing bids for a ship's cook ran as high as three hundred dollars a month, a tremendous salary at that time.

The harbor was jammed with ships abandoned by entire crews who had left for the diggings. Seeing so many deserted vessels was a shock. Passengers received more shock waves after landing. The beach was littered with mirrors, statues, stoves, kegs of coffee, cases of tobacco, cartons of clothing, and crates of cumbersome mining machines. Newcomers soon realized that they, too, had to dump belongings: no porters to serve them; no carriages to move their supplies; no wagons to load their furniture; no servants to care for their clothes.

There were hotels in town where customers slept on wooden planks and tabletops. The hills were covered with tents and shanties because camping out was cheaper and less crowded.

San Francisco grew with incredible speed. Prefabricated houses shipped from China, Europe, and the East Coast were

San Francisco's crowded port

assembled in one day. In 1848, there were approximately eight hundred people in San Francisco. In 1849, there were at least fifteen thousand, and by 1850, twenty-five thousand.[2] San Francisco became an important commercial center. New York and New England merchants profited enormously by sending shiploads of goods needed by gold-hunters who owned little more than a pick and shovel. They advertised their merchandise in newspapers throughout California's gold area.[3]

San Francisco was a stopover, a supply center, and a place to relax. Gambling houses and drinking saloons were everywhere. Streets were strewn with garbage. There were no sanitation or sewage systems. Nevertheless, San Francisco dirt seemed promising to a few people, who idled away their time picking gold flakes in the street—small pickings that

Abandoned ships
were made into
hotels and stores.

probably fell out of miners' bags or were swept from shop-keepers' floors.

All the glitter was bright and encouraging until people noted prices. Inflation was sky-high. Shopkeepers collected gold faster than miners could dig it. Onions and potatoes sold for one dollar each. Eggs were ten dollars a dozen. Tacks were exchanged for their exact weight in gold. A shot of whiskey cost a pinch of gold, and milk cost even more than liquor. Laundry service was so expensive that bundles of dirty clothes were reportedly shipped to China or Hawaii, where they were washed and returned at "$8 a dozen."[4]

Miners returning from the diggings brought in bags, bottles, and buckets of gold. Stories got around about single panfuls of dirt worth two thousand dollars. Treasure was said to be underfoot on land and underwater in streams and rivers. However, many heard that the richest diggings had already been claimed. "There is gold here, but most of the fortunes are obtained, and what is left will require hard and constant labor," one forty-niner wrote.[5] Prospectors headed for the Sierra hills, hoping that depressing reports were deliberately created by successful miners who wanted to discourage competition.

Companies broke up as men decided to try their luck on their own. They didn't want to share the wealth they expected to find. And they wouldn't have to obey leaders,

This merchant claims his food is worth its weight in gold.

Bruff called this sketch "The Midnight Visitor."

abide by laws, and stay with the same crowd. California was not only a land of riches, but also a place of freedom. No officials to stop them, no family to shame them—an ideal place to live without rules.

Diggings were scattered along the western slopes of the Sierra Nevada.[6] *Lode deposits* were in quartz veins deep in the ground. *Placer deposits* consisted of gold dust, flakes, and nuggets scattered through sand and gravel. During the early days of the Gold Rush, placer gold was the only kind known. Picks and shovels were the usual tools for uncovering buried treasure. No need for complex techniques. Just dig until the dirt shows yellow.

Panning in rivers and streams was the simple, popular method. It sounded so easy: Swish a little gravel and water around in a container. A washbasin, laundry tub, basket, or frying pan would do. Then collect the yellow specks that settle in the bottom. But to wash a pan a miner had to squat and keep his hands in icy water. A ton of "dirt" might yield an ounce of gold. It was backbreaking work, especially hard for anyone not used to manual labor. Prospectors often waded knee-deep in water to work. Some used their pants as sacks. They lugged dirt in them by tying the legs of their trousers together.

A *rocker,* also called *cradle,* was quicker than panning. The rocker is a wooden box, open at one end and closed at the other, mounted on rockers. Cleats called "riffles" are nailed to the open end to catch gold. Sand is shoveled in and water

Gold-seekers in the Sierras

Working the Long Tom

poured through while the cradle is rocked violently. A *Long Tom* is an enlarged rocker, eight to twenty feet long. At least three people are needed: one to shovel dirt into it, a second to pour water over the dirt, and a third to rock the big cradle. The Long Tom can handle a lot of dirt, but it needs continuous fast-moving water. This means that miners have to be near a river, or dig a ditch that will bring water to their diggings.

Building a *dam* across a stream sounded sensible. Wall off the water; expose a gold-paved bottom. However, making a dam meant working in freezing waters while carrying

THE GREAT AMERICAN GOLD RUSH

heavy timbers and boulders that were needed for construction. And even these efforts didn't guarantee results.[7] Only a few dams were made in 1849; by 1850, rivers were cluttered with them.

Pans, rockers, and dams weren't needed for a few diving bell enthusiasts. They brought along their gear, put on their metal helmets, and jumped into streams and rivers holding crowbars to pry gold loose. When they sank, their expectations usually did, too.

Dry diggings in ravines and hillsides were usual workplaces. Groups often resorted to *coyoting:* burrowing long tunnels into hills and sinking shafts into the ground. Many people were crushed and killed by cave-ins. Eventually, "coyoters" reinforced tunnels with wood beams.

Finding a fortune was as chancy as picking a winning lottery number. A disheartened, disappointed miner sent this message home: "Say to all my friends: stay at home. Tell my enemies to come."[8]

Housekeeping

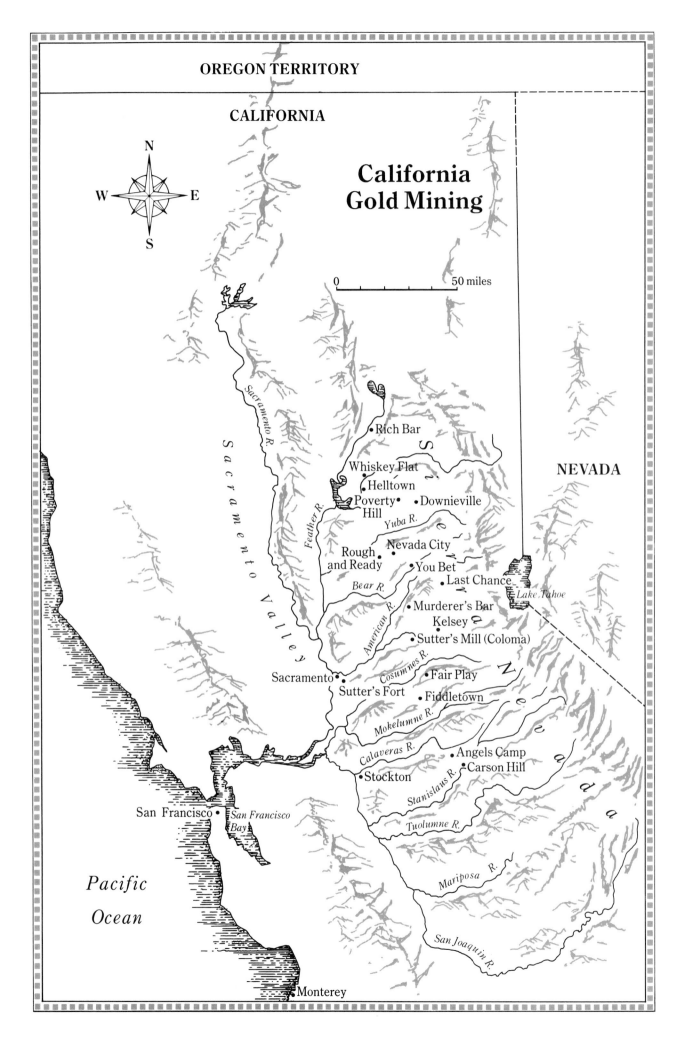

OREGON TERRITORY

CALIFORNIA

California Gold Mining

N
W E
S

0   50 miles

Sacramento R.

Sacramento Valley

Feather R.

• Rich Bar

Whiskey Flat
• Helltown
Poverty •   • Downieville
Hill

Yuba R.

• Nevada City
Rough
and Ready
• You Bet

Bear R.

• Last Chance

Sierra Nevada

NEVADA

Lake Tahoe

• Murderer's Bar
Kelsey

American R.

• Sutter's Mill (Coloma)

Sacramento •
Sutter's Fort •

Cosumnes R.

• Fair Play

• Fiddletown

Mokelumne R.

Calaveras R.

• Angels Camp
• Carson Hill

• Stockton

Stanislaus R.

San Francisco • *San Francisco Bay*

Tuolumne R.

Pacific Ocean

Mariposa R.

San Joaquin R.

• Monterey

7 · AT THE DIGGINGS

ANYONE WHO FOUND GOLD was soon surrounded by other prospectors. When people clustered together, they started new mining camps. Helltown, Angels Camp, Whiskey Flat, Rough and Ready, Last Chance, You Bet, Fiddletown, Murderer's Bar, Fair Play, Poverty Hill, Rich Bar, and hundreds of other places were collections of shabby shacks and tents. These camps were equipped with bars, gambling houses, and stores where miners could spend their gold. New camps appeared as new strikes were made, and were deserted when miners' luck ran out.

No one escaped inflation. At stores near the diggings, prices were sky-high. One forty-niner wrote in his journal that a jar of pickles and two sweet potatoes cost him eleven dollars, and that he paid seven fifty for a needle and thread.[1] Gold dust and nuggets weighed for their value were used instead of currency. But gold by the mule load was true in '48; not after that.[2] Although some struck it rich—and usually kept their finds secret—most prospectors worked hard for an ounce. And an ounce, worth sixteen dollars, wasn't enough to pay for the groceries that Edward Buffum and his friend bought for breakfast. Here is his bill:

"I've had a very good day. I've dug 10,000 francs' worth of gold. I'd like dinner now."
"I'm sorry Sir, I can't cook dinner for less than 15,000 francs!"

One box of sardines	$16
One pound of hard bread	$2
One pound of butter	$6
One half-pound of cheese	$3
Two bottles of ale	$16
Total	$43 [3]

However, no one wanted luxury at the diggings. Get rich; get out; go home. Miners endured all types of hardship, hoping for a grand payoff. Many slept on the cold, wet ground without blankets. Others took the time to set up tents or lean-tos. Those who planned a long stay built cabins. Few bothered to cook anything more complicated than beans or rice. Salt pork, hardtack, and jerked beef were on

Roughing it

the diet. Scurvy was common among miners who neglected
to eat fresh fruit and vegetables.

Keeping clean was a task that took up valuable time. "I
have not had my pants off to sleep since I bin here. I have

The post office in San Francisco, where forty-niners queued daily for letters and newspapers. Some waited in line throughout the night.

not laid on a bed nether," George Cornell wrote to his wife.[4] James Heren revealed that you "shake yourself and you are dressed."[5] Melvin Paden explained why he wore rags. "I do not like to be apacking a thousand dollars about in my coat pocket for it has toar my pockets and puld the Coat to peaces."[6]

Doctors were kept busy tending the sick. There were plenty of legitimate doctors, some borne along with the Gold Rush, others who came out with the sole intention of

THE GREAT AMERICAN GOLD RUSH

serving the sick. Most miners had to travel far to see a physician—and they were often too sick to go anywhere.[7]

Miners died from varieties of ailments, many caused by filth, bad food, too much liquor, and horrible working conditions.[8] Quacks with no medical degrees outnumbered licensed physicians. One of them sold "searching and raking pills," specially designed for diggers with ailments. His prescription contained ordinary flour. Another phony physician instructed men to bury themselves up to their necks in earth so that they could soak up the healing powers of the ground.

"Seeing the elephant" was an expression most often used during the Gold Rush to mean experiencing hardship. Sick miners and disappointed prospectors wrote in letters and diaries that they had "seen the elephant" and were ready to quit the diggings.

The mining season came to an end with the rainy season, which lasted from November to May. Prospecting then was risky because mountain winters were harsh. Most gold-diggers moved to Sacramento, San Francisco, and other large towns for the winter. Boredom and homesickness made socializing important.

OVERLEAF: A miners' dance, by A. Castaigne.

A view of San Francisco in 1851

Gambling

The biggest crowds could be found at gambling houses and drinking saloons. It was a common sight to find men drunk, disorderly, and dead broke. Those who had found pay dirt spent their gold quickly, sure that their luck would hold out. Others, who hadn't found gold, forgot their troubles by spending whatever they had. Many disillusioned miners headed home. After one week at the mines, twenty-year-old William Johnson was disgusted because he earned an average of eight dollars a day. He worked at mining for four months, until he had enough money to get back to Pittsburgh. A Philadelphia teacher named Dan Woods was another disappointed miner. He and some friends had built a dam on the Tuolumne River in order to wash its bed of gold. When the dam broke, his spirits did, too. Woods was happy to return to the schoolroom.

THE GREAT AMERICAN GOLD RUSH

Despite reports of disappointment and hardships, new-comers kept arriving by ship and through overland routes. Newspapers all over the country kept spreading gold fever by publishing letters from miners who had been successful. "Thousands are in high spirits and are making money fast." "Gold does exist in greatest abundance here, and if a man will use industry and economy there is nothing to keep him from making a fortune in a few years at most." "I believe there is a fortune for everyone who will come and get it."[9]

Letters from California emigrants were featured in practically every village and city newspaper. Families and friends were happy to hand editors mail that had the latest news from the West. Published letters of this kind were so sensational that not only would-be miners, but also businessmen hurried west to make money in the new land of opportunity. Most business-minded emigrants came from the Northeast. Collis Huntington from New York was a forty-niner who made a small fortune selling shovels from his store in Sacramento. Mark Hopkins was another New York forty-niner

Saloons attracted gold-seekers from many parts of the world.

THE GREAT AMERICAN GOLD RUSH

Mud covered the streets of San Francisco during the winter of 1849.

who became rich running a hardware store in that city. Both men became famous millionaires.[10]

Torrential rains during the winter of 1849–1850 turned most of Sacramento into one big lake. People waited on roofs or clung to wreckage until boats rescued them. An untold number of people drowned. When the rains ended and waters receded in January, Sacramento was one stinking mudhole. Because it was a major supply center vital to miners and merchants, it was cleaned up and rebuilt quickly.

San Francisco also needed constant rebuilding. Fires were commonplace. City dwellers replaced charred wooden shacks that acted as tinderboxes with brick buildings. Businessmen, who were making enormous profits as a result of the city's incredible growth, also used brick to reconstruct shops, hotels, restaurants, and gambling houses. Despite this, fires kept plaguing San Francisco. Between 1849 and 1851 six major fires destroyed large parts of the city.[11]

The Sacramento flood of January 1850

Not everyone left the diggings during winter. Some people were so obsessed with mining, they couldn't stop. They courted disaster. Some nearly starved to death because there weren't decent roads for transporting food. In early spring, rivers overflowed and flooded diggings. Quite a few miners drowned.

Claims

Because crowds pushed and shoveled to find treasure, claim laws were set. Miners' codes varied from camp to camp. In some places each person's claim was limited to ten feet; in other places there was a fifty-foot limit. If a claim wasn't worked for a week, it was usually considered free for someone else. A miner could hold a claim by leaving his

Three cannons were needed to protect your gold, according to this French cartoon.

tools at his diggings. Camps had claims officers who were paid by miners to patrol mines, settle disputes, and allow the buying and selling of sites.

Swindlers practiced "salting": They scattered gold in the dirt, then sold their claims for thousands of dollars. "Jumping," taking another person's claim, was all too common. Disputes were often settled by a jury of miners, or by a judge chosen for the case.

Mining camps established their own rules. Claims permitted people to dig but didn't give them property rights. Public land could be mined, not owned. But no one cared about owning land anyway.

Claims were limited to one a person. However, some prospectors had others claim sites for them, and so they had multiple holdings. Where no mining camps existed, people claimed vast expanses of land. They even posted notices stating that they had exclusive rights to certain streams. One person who had been prospecting in the mountains put up this sign: "A.B. and company (no telling how large that is) claim this stream up and down."[12]

Disappointed miners who were ready to believe promising tall tales were always on the move. Thousands of diggers went into a frenzy when they heard about the Lake of Gold, with walnut-sized nuggets on its shores and rocks of solid gold under its waters. Indians who camped nearby reportedly used fish hooks and arrowheads of gold. The place was hard to reach, for it was in a deep gorge high up in the mountains. Hordes of prospectors quit working their claims and climbed the Sierra peaks looking for the lake of their dreams.

A man named Stoddard probably started the Lake of Gold myth. He had staggered out of the mountains raving about it. Stoddard declared that he had taken gold from the fabulous lake, but when hostile Indians attacked him, he had to drop everything and flee for his life.

Searching for gold

Seeing the elephant

Using Stoddard as guide, an expedition was immediately organized. The group spent weeks wandering in snow-covered mountains. When Stoddard admitted being lost, men threatened to hang him unless he found the Lake of Gold within twenty-four hours. Before anyone managed to put a noose around Stoddard's neck, he slipped away.[13]

This wild goose chase proved successful for three Germans. While returning from their search for the mythical lake, they discovered cracks and crevices filled with gold. After news about their findings got around, diggers swarmed around them, and the mining town of Rich Bar was founded.

THE GREAT AMERICAN GOLD RUSH

Six months after the '49 Lake of Gold fiasco, prospectors were electrified by reports of a seashore with sands of gold. Called Gold Bluffs, the fabulous beach was said to stretch for miles beneath gorgeous bluffs, near the Oregon border. The only bother was taking out specks of black that dotted the gold sand. During 1850 and 1851 hundreds of prospectors went to Gold Bluffs. J. Goldsborough Bruff was among them. He found "many bones of whales . . . and Numerous skate-fish, star-fish &c."—but no treasure.[14]

In January 1851, California emigrants organized the Pacific Mining Company. A newspaper reported that "the secretary of the Pacific Mining Company measured a patch of gold and sand, and estimates it will yield to *each* member of the company the snug little sum of $43,000,000." The newspaper account went on to state that $43 million was an understatement. Profit could be ten times more![15]

The precious beach was never found. Legend had led thousands astray.

8 · LAW AND ORDER

VIOLENCE AND CRIME were commonplace when swarms of armed gold-seekers collided with one another during their search for riches. Much of the trouble was caused by people who had criminal records before they came to California. Thieves, holdup men, and killers got away with murder. "Yesterday one American shot another in the street," one emigrant noted, "and the occurrence was not noticed as much as a dog fight at home."[1] After listing six murders within seven days another wrote, "It is surprising how indifferent people become to the sight of violence and bloodshed in this country."[2]

However, most people in California were horrified by the lawlessness. They blamed their military governors. Army officers who had been in charge of the government since the Mexican War ended in 1848 couldn't control crime. Editors and public speakers protested against military rule and called for reforms.

In 1849, Californians chose forty-eight delegates for a constitutional convention, which was held in Monterey. The delegates drafted and ratified a state constitution that provided for elected officials and for courts of law. They also voted to outlaw slavery.

When delegates petitioned Congress to admit California

as a state in the Union, Southerners were in an uproar. They refused to admit another free state. Southern congressmen were so riled that they threatened to secede from the Union, and a few of them shouted that the time was ripe for civil war against the North. Northerners were disturbed not only because of the slavery issue, but also because they had important business interests in both the South and in California. They needed to protect their trade rights and their investments, and they wanted the new, rich California on their side. The outcome of the California issue was critical to the future of the United States. After months of long, impassioned outbursts, an agreement was reached. Congress passed the Compromise of 1850. Although it admitted California as a slave-free state, Southerners were appeased because the

This parade in San Francisco celebrated California's statehood.

THE GREAT AMERICAN GOLD RUSH

compromise included a new, strict Fugitive Slave Law.[3]

Californians were ecstatic about their statehood. They staged parades and parties to celebrate the historic event. But despite elected officials and established courts of law, crime couldn't be controlled. There were too many dishonest elections, corrupt judges, and rigged juries, and not enough police. At most camps, there were no police and no courts.

Miners established their own forms of justice. Arrest, trial, and punishment could take but a few hours. No time to waste on criminals, and no place to keep them. Verdicts could be decided by popular vote, or by a judge and jury quickly set up for the case.

There were five popular types of punishment.

Banishment: An undesirable character who had caused trouble by jumping a claim or attacking someone was warned to leave the diggings and never return.

Cutting off ears: Wearing long hair was especially popular among earless felons.

Branding: A hot iron caused a permanent scar. (On the North Fork of the American River a man who stole three hundred dollars had his ears cut off and the letter *T* branded on his cheek.)[4]

Flogging: An ordinary means of punishment. Lashings with whips were used by the army and navy at that time. A man who stole ninety-eight pounds of gold received a hundred lashes, and his ears were cut off.[5]

Hanging: The death sentence applied for robberies as well as murders. (Two New Englanders found with stolen horses weren't tried. They were "condemned by acclamation" by a mob, then hanged.[6])

Lynchings were all too common. Crowds out of control grabbed suspects and hanged them without trials. Watching a scaffold being built and witnessing a victim swinging by the neck were often viewed as forms of entertainment.

A mining town judge hears a case.

THE GREAT AMERICAN GOLD RUSH

The first of the Gold Rush hangings occurred in January 1849. After receiving thirty-nine lashes each for alleged stealing, two Frenchmen and one Chilean were accused of crimes that had taken place the year before. As a result of the flogging, they were too weak to defend themselves. They couldn't understand the charges anyway, because they did not understand English. A mob hanged them, and it threatened to hang the New Englander, Edward Buffum, who mounted a stump and tried in vain to stop the proceedings "in the name of God, humanity, and law."[7]

Mob decisions were common, but in many instances miners' courts meted out "justice." Louise Clappe described the proceedings of a trial by jury. A judge and a jury of twelve had been chosen. After only a few minutes' deliberation there was a verdict: "That William Brown, convicted of stealing, etc., should be *one hour* from that time, be hung by the neck until he was dead." The sentence was immediately altered to be more lenient. The prisoner was given *three hours* before being hanged. It gave him time to write a farewell letter to his family in Sweden.[8]

Another barbaric lynching took place at Downieville on July 5, 1851. A Mexican woman named Juanita was seen arguing with John Cannon, a Scottish miner. She stabbed him to death. Juanita claimed self-defense against a drunken miner who had tried to force himself into her shack. Within minutes an infuriated mob seized her and brought her to the town square for instant trial. A lawyer who tried to defend her was knocked down and beaten. Juanita adjusted the noose around her own neck while a maddened mob of thousands watched a unique show: the execution of a female. Before Juanita was hanged, her skirts were tied around her legs—for modesty's sake. She was the only woman hanged in a mining town.

Robberies and murders were daily occurrences in San Francisco. Crime was out of control: only a handful of

Hangings were public events.

policemen, no adequate jails or courts. People were terrorized by hoodlums. A gang called the Regulators, also known as the Hounds, held drunken parades, careening around the streets armed with brass knuckles and slingshots. They raided shops, broke into homes, extorted money from businesses, provoked fights, and roughed up foreigners.

One night in July 1849, they attacked a Chilean neighborhood. They burned tents, assaulted men and women, and shot at the feet of those who tried to run away. Law-abiding people were so horrified that they donated money to help rebuild the Chileans' homes, and they insisted that officials arrest the Hounds. After a proper trial, eight were found guilty. They were exiled because there were no jails.

Criminal gangs called the Sydney Ducks also terrorized San Franciscans. They were predominantly made up of ex-convicts and escaped convicts from Australia. Some people suspected that fires had been deliberately set by gangs who were intent upon looting property from burned-out buildings. (Although arson may have taken place in some instances, San Francisco's tent and wood buildings were fuel for fires caused by careless accidents.)

Because the government could not control crime, some citizens decided to take the law into their own hands. In 1851 they organized a committee of vigilance, "for the protection of the lives and property of the citizens and residents of the City of San Francisco."[9] Their methods of dispensing justice were shocking. They conducted hasty trials and passed sentences in secret. Witnesses and lawyers for defendants were usually afraid to appear. One man who stole a small safe was brought before the Vigilantes and hanged within a few hours before a cheering, jeering crowd. According to the Vigilantes, thieves deserved the same fate as murderers—and there was no sense wasting time with lawyers or long trials.

The Vigilantes made eighty-nine arrests. They hanged

four men, flogged one, banished twenty-eight, turned fifteen over to authorities, and released forty-one. Prominent businessmen were among the hundreds of members of the Vigilantes. Praised by newspapers of the time, the group actually did little to ensure true justice. Although the Vigilantes did reduce crime, many of their actions were appalling because they judged and lynched victims who had no legal means of defending themselves.[10]

The Vigilantes of 1851 disbanded after a hundred days—and as soon as two of its members were elected to the state legislature. However, do-it-yourself justice was still part of the Gold Rush scene. Sacramento, Stockton, and Los Angeles also had vigilante groups.

Vigilante groups continued to form throughout the 1850s. This scene depicts an 1856 double hanging.

9 · FOREIGNERS

$\mathbf{D}$URING THE FIRST YEARS of the Gold Rush, elation and expectations of wealth were so high that people enjoyed working side by side with foreigners. But after 1850, prejudices were so strong that "outsiders" from Mexico, South America, Europe, and Asia were banned from certain camps. They were looked down upon as unworthy of American gold found on American soil. According to some, riches of the land belonged exclusively to United States citizens. Even native American Indians were resented and chased from diggings. Prejudices were voiced by the loud clamors of a few, who felt contempt for anyone who wasn't a native white American citizen.

The Chinese

Silk-gowned merchants who arrived in San Francisco during the first years of the Gold Rush were welcomed in San Francisco as the "celestial men of commerce." Newspapers described them as "useful, quiet, good citizens . . . deserving the respect of all."[1] They were praised as being honest, efficient, and orderly. Chinese merchants imported

Chinese crowded aboard ships that were headed for San Francisco.

grain, rice, sugar, tea, and dried fruits from their country. "Were it not for the Chinese we might have starved the first year," a forty-niner wrote in his diary.[2] The Chinese also brought over textiles, tools, and prefabricated houses that were shipped in sections and assembled in towns and mining camps. A French reporter pronounced these movable houses "the prettiest, the best-made and the cheapest."[3]

In addition to prosperous merchants who had come to conduct businesses, peasant gold-seekers crossed over six thousand miles of rough Pacific waters in crude junks. Most of them were poor farmers and fishermen who had been lured by tales of "gold mountains" in California. As soon as they landed, they hurried to various diggings. Long lines of Chinese made their way through mountain passes, balancing heavy loads on their bamboo poles. They were hospitable, polite, quiet, clean, and called "quaint."

In 1850 there were only a few hundred Chinese in California. Within two years there were twenty thousand. As their numbers grew, and when finding good claims became difficult, "John Chinaman," the "heathen," was resented and banned from many mining camps. "Neither Asiatics nor South Sea Islanders [Hawaiians] shall be allowed to mine in this district" was a typical regulation.[4]

For self-protection against prejudiced ruffians, and also because they worked together efficiently, Chinese established their own mining camps. They were hardworking laborers who could extract gold from claims that had been abandoned by others. "The Chinese waterwheel," which involved buckets on rope pulleys, enabled them to drain streams and uncover gold. Some of the Chinese had worked in the gold fields of Borneo, others at the tin mines of Malaysia. They knew mining techniques, and succeeded where others failed. Their success caused envy and hate. Typical complaints were that they had come to California merely for gold, that nobody benefited from them because they took their money back to Asia.

We used to think 'twould always
last with perfect ease
If Uncle Sam had only stopped
the coming of the Chinese

was a stanza of a popular Gold Rush ballad.[5]

A Chinese mining camp

Spanish-Speaking People

Although many American gold-seekers enjoyed the companionship of foreigners, prejudiced people were intent upon chasing away anyone who wasn't a United States citizen. Mexicans who had come north in huge numbers were resented, especially by miners who were veterans of the Mexican War. They still hated their former enemies. Bias also existed against "Californios," the Spanish-speaking people of California who became United States citizens after the war.

Chileans were also disdained. Together with Mexicans they dominated the southern mines in 1849 and 1850. Many of them were successful because they had worked as miners before. They knew how to separate gold from gravel by *winnowing:* shaking blankets filled with dirt until only gold remained. They also knew how to build stone wheel mills for grinding ore, and they were expert at tunnel and shaft mining. In many places rich Mexicans and South Americans

Mexicans breaking quartz, hoping to find gold inside

THE GREAT AMERICAN GOLD RUSH

South Americans sifting dirt for gold

brought servants to dig for them. This was considered unfair competition.

Grumblers who resented all Spanish-speaking people called them "greasers" and "dangerous in character." They protested that only "free and enlightened citizens" should have the right to mineral wealth in the United States. According to rumor, at least $20 million in gold dust was being shipped to Mexico and South America.

As a result, in 1850 a Foreign Miners' Tax was passed by the California legislature. The law stated that all foreign miners had to pay a monthly license fee of twenty dollars. Those who refused to pay would be arrested. The tax was a "small bonus for the privilege of taking from our country the vast treasure to which they have no right."[6]

There were protest marches by Europeans as well as Mexicans and South Americans. Special vigilante guards accompanied and protected tax collectors—who concentrated on "greasers" and "pigtails" (Chinese), the prime targets of hate. Fearing violence, thousands quit the mines and went home. According to an August 1850 issue of the San Francisco *Evening Picayune,* "from fifteen to 20,000 Mexicans, and perhaps an equal number of *chilenos* [Chileans] are now leaving or preparing to leave California for their own country."[7]

Indians

According to some settlers and emigrants, there were two types of California Indian: One was "wild" and "untameable," the other "useful" and "domesticated." The wild ones, shameless in their nakedness, were like animals, and they were fair game to shoot. The "useful" Indians served settlers by working on the ranches and farms. Their labor was especially valued by emigrants who hired hundreds of them to work as miners.

Sutter was not unique in his attitude toward "his" Indians. Other ranchers used natives as though they were personal slaves. After gold was discovered in 1848, they marched gangs of them to the diggings. Sutter did just that, though in his case he didn't find a fortune. He then leased his Indians to others, on condition that he receive 50 percent of the gold. Even that arrangement didn't make him rich.

Using Indian workers resulted in huge profits. In many instances, their pay consisted of food and coarse clothing. According to one emigrant, Indian workers could be hired for "a mere trifle. They generally contrive to get a shirt and a few get rich enough to buy a coat and pantaloons."[8] James Savage, who once worked at Sutter's fort, used Indians to dig for him. He traded equal weights of goods for gold. For example, a pound of raisins was exchanged for one pound of gold; a three-pound blanket was equal to three pounds of

California Indians

gold. According to one Texan, Savage's Indians "numbering thousands, were earliest in prospecting and finding the shiny metal."[9] Another argonaut estimated that Savage's gold was worth close to half a million dollars.

Some Indians were permitted to prospect on their own. But when they cashed in their finds they were often cheated. A special "Indian ounce," also called a "Digger ounce," was lightweight, worth half its usual value.

Of all racial minorities in California, the Indians suffered most. William Swain, of Youngstown, New York, wrote that there were miners who "had rather shoot an Indian than a deer at any time."[10] Natives who weren't "domesticated" were viewed as obstacles to progress, not only because they occupied land that might have value, but also because they were dangerous "savages." The native American Indian was viewed as a trespasser who had no rights on United States property.

It did not occur to miners who killed game, muddied streams, ruined fishing, and felled trees that they were destroying supplies that natives needed for survival. Robbed of their resources, Indians frequently stole and butchered emigrants' cattle and raided miners' camps for supplies. Occasionally they deliberately attacked white intruders who were destroying their way of life.

According to California's 1849 constitution, Indians had no political nor legal rights. They were foreigners on United States property who could not own land or expect protection from attack. Only "white male citizens" could vote. The following year, the Law of 1850 proclaimed further rulings. It did state that whites must treat Indians "humanely." That meant that employers were obligated to feed and clothe them. Should they neglect to do so, they would be fined "no less than $10." However, any Indian who seemed idle could be arrested and jailed until some white employer volunteered to hire him.

There were people who were shocked at the plight of the Indian. They protested, wanting reforms that would enable native Americans to live in freedom, with dignity. But the loudest, strongest voices of the time were in favor of some solution to what was called "the Indian problem." Three commissioners appointed by the federal government concluded that the choice was between "extermination or domestication."[11] Either kill them or set them up in reservations, where they could become "civilized."

All across America Indians who were in the way were usually sent to reservations located west of their home territory. The dilemma in California was that only ocean was west, and it was unthinkable to send Indians east. California's first governor, Peter H. Burnett, stated that "a war of extermination will continue to be waged . . . until the Indian race becomes extinct."[12] During the nineteenth century thousands of Indians were hunted down and killed.

Blacks

In 1848 blacks were among the first miners. Like other crew members, black seamen (mainly from New England whalers) jumped ship to seek gold. Freed slaves, fugitives, and gangs of "negro servants" brought by Southerners increased their numbers to about two thousand by 1852—only about 1 percent of the population of California.

California held a powerful attraction for blacks, who hoped that gold would enable them to buy freedom for themselves and their families. In some instances, slaves received their masters' permission to leave. Their return seemed guaranteed, because they had left their wives and children behind.

Alvin Coffey, a slave from Missouri, dug up five thousand

dollars' worth of gold for his master. Then he was sold to another Missourian. After unearthing large profits, Coffey paid thousands of dollars to free himself, his wife, and two daughters. James Taylor, from Ohio, already freed by his master, managed to dig up enough to buy freedom for his wife and seven children before he returned home.

Slaveholders from the South often brought their staff to work in the mines. General Thomas Jefferson Green, a rich Texan, filed claims not only in his own name, but also in the names of his slaves. Infuriated miners called a meeting and passed a resolution excluding blacks from the area.

The Fugitive Slave Law of 1850, providing for the return between states of escaped slaves, was a threat to those blacks who had found refuge in the North. Many of them looked to California as a haven, since it was so out of the way that their capture would be difficult. Because California had been established as a free state, they hoped for sympathy and understanding. However, "persons of color" weren't always welcome, and they were sometimes chased from the diggings.

Fortunately, there were argonauts like Scotsman William Downie, whose group consisted of seven blacks and two white men. They worked in harmony and were rewarded with rich diggings. The prosperous town of Downieville was named in the Scotsman's honor.

There were other groups like Downie's in Gold Rush country.

10 · WOMEN

MINERS SUFFERED from loneliness and lack of love. They yearned for the affections of the "gentler sex." Hundreds of girls from France and South America were among the first prostitutes to come to California. Chinese, Australian, and American "soiled doves" competed with them for business in San Francisco, Sacramento, and other large settlements. Some were dance-hall girls who found customers at bars and gambling houses. Others worked in brothels under "bosses" who occasionally sent them on road tours of nearby mining towns. With the exception of wives who came with their husbands, "respectable ladies" were hard to find. Miners pined for them and wrote home about their yearnings for "proper, honest women."[1]

Eliza Farnham, formerly a matron for prisoners at Sing Sing Prison in New York State, determined to correct the shocking situation in California. She sent a letter to the New York *Tribune* about her plan to escort "intelligent, virtuous and efficient women" to the West, noting that "there are hundreds, if not thousands of such females in our country who are not bound by any tie." Qualified females had to be at least twenty-five years old, in good health, and ready to submit character references "from their clergyman or some authority of the town where they reside."[2] The charge of

$250 per lady would be worthwhile if it led to marital bliss. Mrs. Farnham engaged a ship, aptly named the *Angelique,* scheduled to sail April 15, 1850, with 130 pure maidens. To ensure safe, virtuous passage, she and "six or eight respectable married men and their families" would escort her precious girls.[3] Newspapers praised her noble plan as an "errand of mercy," and when California bachelors read about it, they dreamed of the good ship *Angelique* and its cargo of delights.

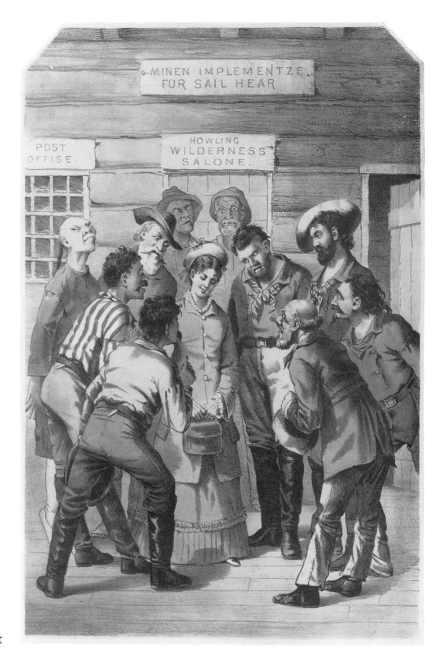

Gawking at a rare sight

But Mrs. Farnham was more successful as a prison matron than as a matchmaker. Although several hundred women inquired about her plan, only three females accompanied her—a terrible disappointment for the lonely hearts in California. After observing the habits of Western life, however,

THE GREAT AMERICAN GOLD RUSH

Mrs. Farnham declared she was glad her plan had failed, because California society did not deserve "the higher order of female intelligence."[4] According to her, it wasn't suitable for respectable women.

A few unattached girls went west on their own, hoping to pick and choose husbands from love-starved men. Some waited to set out until they received marriage proposals by mail. Others advertised their qualifications in newspapers. Here is an ad that may have been published as a joke, to make fun of serious ads placed by single women:

A HUSBAND WANTED

By a lady who can wash, cook, scour, sew, milk, spin, weave, hoe (can't plow), cut wood, make fires, feed the pigs, raise children, rock the cradle (golden rocker, I thank you Sir!), saw a plank, drive nails, . . . paint houses, white-wash fences, &c.

Now for her terms.

Her age is none of your business. She is neither handsome nor a fright, yet an *old* man need *not* apply . . . there must be $20,000 settled on her before she will bind herself.[5]

However, marriage wasn't the main reason women came to California. Some expected to mine gold, and quite a few wanted to start businesses. Many restaurants and boarding-houses were all-female enterprises. Luzena Wilson served meals to hundreds of miners in Nevada City, California, charging them each twenty-five dollars a week. She also became their banker, storing their gold dust in milk pails and also under her mattress.[6] Margaret Frink was another who answered the siren call of gold. She opened a hotel in Sacramento and made enough money to order from the East Coast a "cottage," which was shipped to California by way of Cape Horn.[7]

A woman brings lunch to three miners.

THE GREAT AMERICAN GOLD RUSH

Throughout the Gold Rush years there weren't many women at mining camps. Living among rough, uncouth men wasn't appropriate for females of the 1850s, who had been brought up to be delicate, sheltered creatures. When Louise Clappe dutifully and reluctantly joined her physician husband at Rich Bar, her friends were shocked. "Some said that I ought to be in a strait jacket," she wrote, "for I was undoubtedly mad . . . that I should never get there alive . . . that even if the Indians did not kill me, I should expire of ennui [boredom] or cold." The prospect of a respectable woman living among male miners was called "absolutely indelicate."[8]

Much to everyone's surprise, Louise Clappe loved the "wild and barbarous life" of a mining camp. Elated by the beautiful mountain surroundings and fascinated by events at the diggings, she wrote detailed accounts about "nature's great lottery scheme" in letters to her sister.[9]

She described the few women at Rich Bar. One, a "gigantic piece of humanity," had carried fifty pounds of flour on her back while trudging through five feet of snow. Another, "a gentle and amiable looking woman, about twenty five years of age," had endured an agonizing overland crossing with a sick husband and three small children. A widow whose husband had died of cholera on an overland trail supported ten children by taking in laundry and ironing clothes "on a chair in the open air." Her home was a covered wagon.[10]

Mrs. Clappe lived in a log cabin with comparative elegance. She even had tableware. One time a neighbor having a dinner party declined her offer to lend him knives, forks, and spoons because he said that his guests might feel he was "putting on airs." He borrowed one spoon, which was passed around the table for all to use.

Catherine Haun was another woman who dared to live at a mining camp. This newlywed from Iowa eagerly traveled overland with her husband, expecting to dig for gold to pay off debts. She also hoped that a change of climate would improve her poor health. (A "change of air" was commonly prescribed for any illness. Many emigrants traveled west on doctors' orders.) Like other women on the trail, Catherine collected dried buffalo dung for fuel, built campfires, helped push and lift wagons, and engaged in many other "unladylike labors." Despite the drudgery, Catherine enjoyed the journey, especially because she looked forward

Women traveling overland with their families

THE GREAT AMERICAN GOLD RUSH

to California, where she anticipated dressing in style. She had packed a lace-trimmed bonnet and an elaborate silk gown to be worn "when I should make my first appearance upon the golden streets of the mining town in which we might locate."[11]

Whether mining, housekeeping, hiking, yoking or driving oxen, pitching tents, or loading wagons, women usually wore ankle-length dresses. Some daring females wore mens' pants and straddled horses instead of riding sidesaddle, which was the accepted ladylike way. Caring for babies and pregnancy, a "condition" impolite to mention, were not considered reasons for delaying travel.[12]

A growing number of women and children arrived after 1850. By that time, land crossings at Panama and Nicaragua were more comfortable, and the journey could be made in three or four weeks. Some wives went west at their husbands' suggestion; others headed out because they were lonely and were determined to track down the men who had left them. Single women also joined the migration because California *was* a land of opportunity where a woman could earn her own living and become independent.[13]

California was the first state to allow separate property rights for married women. Everything a woman owned before marriage, or acquired afterwards, remained hers. In other states a wife's property belonged to the husband. One sponsor of this liberal law declared that it would benefit the state because women—especially the wealthy ones—would be encouraged to settle in California.

11 · THE END OF THE RAINBOW

THE MAD RUSH CONTINUED through the 1850s and reached its peak in 1852, the year miners dug up over $81 million in gold. After that the heyday of the lone prospector was over. Most of the surface gold had been taken. Shovelers could no longer find pay dirt, and panners' efforts didn't "pan out." It was frustrating to sight massive veins of rock, peppered with specks of gold—treasure you could see and feel, but couldn't get at. Shafts were sunk, but heavy machinery was needed to grind up rock and extract gold. *Quartz mining,* also called *hardrock mining,* required expensive equipment that only big businesses could afford.

A pot of gold at the end of the rainbow was real for quite a few adventurers. Using a spoon, a Californian called Chino Tirador loaded a tray with gold that was almost more than he could lift. Mr. Brookmire, who pushed his wheelbarrow from coast to coast, returned to his home in Pennsylvania with fifteen thousand dollars in treasure. Sergeant Carson, the young dreamer who had envisioned castles of marble and multitudes of maidens, didn't find enough gold to make his fantasies come true. But Carson Creek and Carson Hill were named in his honor because he discovered pay dirt there. He was elated by his success. Gold worth millions was mined

Devil's Gate,
sketched by Bruff

from Carson Hill—after he left. A chunk weighing 195 pounds was dislodged from Carson Hill in 1854. It was the largest single nugget ever discovered in California.

J. Goldsborough Bruff failed to find gold, but he didn't come home empty-handed. His notebooks, filled with drawings and details of his adventures, are Gold Rush treasures. Bruff returned to his wife and five children after an absence of over two years and resumed his job in Washington, D.C., as a government draftsman. Quite a few other disillusioned miners quit the diggings as soon as they had enough money to pay for passage home. However, many ex-gold-seekers found jobs, remained in California, and sent for their families.

More merchants than miners struck it rich because the needs of emigrants and the growth of cities had created a new, huge market. Here's an example of a poor peddler who became a millionaire merchant: Levi Strauss eked out a living in New York City selling pots, pans, and other items door-to-door. He jumped at a chance to set sail for the West when his sister offered to pay his way, and he took along bolts of tenting material. When he arrived in San Francisco, he decided that the canvas would make the sturdiest trousers a miner could use. He made Levi pants, and filled his own pockets with gold. Charles Crocker was another lucky businessman. After leaving home in Indiana and crossing the plains, he opened a general store in Sacramento. Crocker eventually became one of the country's richest men.

Ludwig Schliemann left a successful banking business in Germany to set himself up in Sacramento as a buyer of gold. Unfortunately, he died of typhus. His brother Heinrich journeyed from Russia to California to take over the business. "My bank is jammed, crammed, and rammed full of people from different nations and I have to speak all day long in eight languages," he wrote in his diary.[1] (He spoke to customers in English, Russian, German, French, Dutch, Spanish, Italian, and Portuguese.) Heinrich Schliemann amassed a small fortune and, after a ten-month stay, he returned to Europe. This financial wizard became world famous as the archaeologist who uncovered the ancient city of Troy.

The man who discovered the first nugget never made money. After squatters forced James Marshall to abandon his claims near the sawmill, he tried his luck mining in other places. But he couldn't spot a glimmer of gold. To bolster his ego he claimed supernatural powers that enabled him to find treasure. Gullible miners wanted him to lead them to rich gold deposits, and when he refused, they threatened to lynch him. He had to flee for his life. Marshall ended up working as a blacksmith in Kelsey, California. He died poor in 1885.

The Gold Rush was also a calamity for John Sutter, who

had said that he expected to be "the richest, wealthiest man on the Pacific Shore."[2] After his empire New Helvetia was sold to pay his debts, Sutter moved to a beautiful farm on the Feather River, in Gold Rush country. Floods damaged his fields and gardens. When his house was destroyed by fire in 1866, he left California and moved east to a modest home in Lititz, Pennsylvania. Sutter spent most of his time and money trying to establish legal ownership of New Helvetia. He stayed in Washington whenever Congress was in session, hoping the government would listen to his sad story and reward him with land grants. However, Congress rejected his requests. He died in 1880 during one of his stays in Washington.

Before 1850 many prospectors earned up to a hundred dollars a day digging for themselves or working for others.

A popular banking house

THE GREAT AMERICAN GOLD RUSH

A few lucky miners made fortunes. However, although one quarter of a billion dollars' worth of gold was dug up between 1848 and 1852, most argonauts never found treasure in the earth. The Gold Rush was a great gamble that produced lots of losers and only a few winners.

California mines yielded fabulous amounts of gold that flowed into circulation not only in America, but also in Europe. Between 1848 and 1852, California's population increased from 15,000 to 250,000. Its astonishing growth created an enormous world market that brought profits especially to America's industrialized Northeast and to European exporters of manufactured goods.

As a result of the Gold Rush, the United States became one of the richest, most powerful nations in the world. Its wealth was measured not only by its gold-filled treasury, but also by its vast, valuable lands that stretched across a continent.

During the 1850s traveling to the coast became easier. Large ocean liners using the Cape Horn route brought thousands of Europeans and Americans to California. Fine sailing ships and steamers offered comfortable passage to Panama or Nicaragua and then to San Francisco. Overland trails became well-traveled with stopovers, supply stations, and settlements along the way.

Going west was no longer an adventure confined to pioneers, frontiersmen, and farmers. It was also a goal for businesspeople and city folk who wanted to settle in or near cities like Sacramento and San Francisco. Agriculture in valleys flourished, and industry in cities boomed. Even after the day of the lone prospector was over, people came west in droves, lured by the beauty of the land, the challenge of adventure, the chance to start a new career, and the prospect of a better life-style. Emigrants were no longer lured by gold, but by golden opportunities.

Most of the illustrations Rhoda Blumberg has selected date back to the Gold Rush years. Books, magazines, and newspapers of the time often depicted travel and mining conditions. Cartoons that appeared in newspapers and magazines lampooned the symptoms and consequences of gold fever. Although hundreds of gold-seekers kept diaries, only a few illustrated their notes. J. Goldsborough Bruff was the most skilled. His sketches provide vivid glimpses of an American argonaut's experiences.

Illustration on page 12 courtesy of the American Antiquarian Society, Worcester, Massachusetts; page 103 courtesy of the American Museum of Natural History, department of library services, painting by Arthur A. Jansson under the direction of Clark Wissler, photo by H. S. Rice; pages 4, 5, 15, 24, 27, 33, 35, 36, 61, 73, 85, 97, and 110 courtesy of the Bancroft Library, University of California at Berkeley; pages 49 and 118 sketches by J. Goldsborough Bruff and pages 72 and 84 courtesy of the Beinecke Rare Book and Manuscript Library, Yale University; pages 2 and 3 courtesy of the California Department of Parks and Recreation; pages 25 and 86 courtesy of the California Historical Society Library, the Photographic Archives; pages viii, 7, 63, 69, 82–83, 93, 109, and 112 courtesy of the California State Library, California Section; page 45, lithograph by Franklin R. Grist, and page 114 courtesy of Denver Public Library, western history department; pages 51, 52, 54, 58, 66, and 95 courtesy of the Henry E. Huntington Library and Art Gallery; page 19 courtesy of the Historical Society of York County, Pennsylvania; pages 10, 48, and 120 courtesy of the Library of Congress; page 38 courtesy of the Mariners Museum, Newport News, Virginia; page 67 watercolor by William McIlvaine courtesy of Museum of Fine Arts, Boston, M. and M. Karolik Collection; page 11 detail of William Sidney Mount's *California News,* courtesy of the Museums at Stony Brook, Gift of Mr. and Mrs. Ward Melville, 1955; pages 9, 13, 14, 100, and 101, pages 29 and 30 lithograph by N. Currier, 43, 65, 68, 79, and 92 lithographs by Francis (Frank) Samuel Marryat, 117 courtesy of the New-York Historical Society, New York City; page 74 tinted lithograph by H. F. Cox and page 75 chromolithograph by Francis (Frank) Samuel Marryat, courtesy of the New York Public Library, Astor, Lenox and Tilden Foundations, the Print Collection, Miriam and Ira D. Wallach Division of Art, Prints and Photographs; page 59 courtesy of the United States Department of the Interior, National Park Service, Scotts Bluff National Monument; page 44 detail of A. F. Miller's *Sioux Indian Guard* and page 50 *Fort Laramie* by Alfred Jacob Miller courtesy of Walters Art Gallery, Baltimore; pages 8, 16, 23, 41, 57, 64, 76–77, 78, 80–81, 89, 90, 99, and 107 courtesy of Wells Fargo Bank.

NOTES

CHAPTER 1. GOLD FEVER

1. As a result of the treaty, the United States paid $15 million for more than 525,000 square miles of land (now Arizona, western Colorado, Nevada, New Mexico, Texas, Utah, part of Wyoming, and California). The Rio Grande and the Gila River denoted the boundary between the United States and Mexico.

2. Sutter was unsuccessful operating a farm in Missouri. He became a trader in Santa Fe, then a trader in the Rocky Mountain area, but he couldn't make a living. After joining a fur trapping company, he worked in the Northwest, then sailed to Hawaii, where he seems to have idled away his time for five months, until he found a ship bound for California.

3. Oscar Lewis, *Sutter's Fort: Gateway to the Gold Fields* (Englewood Cliffs, N.J.: Prentice-Hall, 1966), 83.

4. *Ibid.,* 145. (Although January 24, 1848, is usually indicated as the day Marshall discovered gold, the exact date is open to question.)

5. J. S. Holliday, *The World Rushed In: The California Gold Rush Experience* (New York: Simon & Schuster, 1981), 33.

6. William Weber Johnson, *The Forty-Niners* (Alexandria, Va.: Time-Life Books, 1974), 17.

7. *Ibid.,* 29.

8. Everyone, including the captain, abandoned a Hudson's Bay ship, and sailors of the *Flora* mutinied and refused to set sail. See John Walton Caughey, *The California Gold Rush* (Berkeley and Los Angeles: University of California Press, 1973), 21.

9. The estimated population of San Francisco in 1848 was eight hundred to nine hundred. When Colonel Mason, the military governor, visited San Francisco on August 20, 1848, "all, or nearly all, its male inhabitants had gone to the mines." (Quote is from his official report to Washington.)

10. Walter Colton, *Three Years in California* in *California Gold, Selected Source Materials for College Research Papers* by Edwin Bingham (Boston: Heath and Company, 1959), 2.

11. *Ibid.*

12. Holliday, 35.

13. *Ibid.*

14. *Ibid.,* 42.

15. E. Gould Buffum, *Six Months in the Gold Mines* in Bingham, 15.

16. Holliday, 40.

17. *Ibid.,* 48.

CHAPTER 2. THE FEVER SPREADS

1. Holliday, 55.
2. Johnson, 43.
3. Holliday, 45.
4. *Ibid.,* 56.
5. Donald Dale Jackson, *Gold Dust* (Lincoln, Nebr.: University of Nebraska Press, 1980), 88.
6. *Ibid.,* 71.
7. Henry Simpson, *Three Weeks in the Gold Mines, or Adventures with the Diggers of California Gold* (New York: Joyce & Co., 1848), 16.
8. Stewart S. White, *The Forty-Niners* (New Haven, Conn.: Yale University Press, 1921), 64.
9. Prefabricated houses were brought over from Europe, New England, and China. These put-together-take-apart structures were set up in mining towns and in California cities.
10. As early as May 15, 1848, French consul Jacques Moerenhout, who had visited gold mines in California, sent nuggets to his government and urged them to send prospectors. Before the Gold Rush was over at least thirty thousand Frenchmen had come to California. France benefited. By 1851 French miners had sent four hundred million francs to their homeland. (See Introduction to *Gold Seeker: Adventures of a Belgian Argonaut During the Gold Rush Years* by Jean-Nicolas Perlot.)

CHAPTER 3. SHORTCUTS: PANAMA, NICARAGUA, MEXICO

1. George W. Groh, *Gold Fever: Being a True Account, Both Horrifying and Hilarious of the Art of Healing (so-called) During the California Gold Rush* (New York: William Morrow, 1966), 30.
2. John Letts, "Across the Isthmus" in *The Course of Empire* by Valeska Bari (New York: Coward-McCann, 1931), 179.
3. Cholera was brought into New York and New Orleans ports in 1848 by ships from Europe carrying passengers afflicted with the disease. This deadly contagion traveled across the country and across the border to Mexico, Panama, and South America. The outbreak took more lives than any previous epidemic in American history. The cause of the disease was a mystery until 1883, when German scientist Robert Koch identified the infecting bacteria.
4. After 1850 a steamer, the *Orus,* was available for river travel as an alternative to bungos—for those who could afford passage.
5. Bayard Taylor, *Eldorado or Adventures in the Path of Empire* (New York: Alfred A. Knopf, 1949), 23.
6. "I was well satisfied to leave Panama at the time: the cholera, which had already carried off one fourth of the native population, was making havoc among Americans." Taylor, 25.
7. Prejudice against Peruvian passengers caused such a commotion that General Persifer Smith, who was on his way to head the army in California, issued a circular stating that foreigners had no right carrying off gold belonging to the United States.
8. Groh, 57.

9. Travel through Nicaragua didn't become popular until 1851, when millionaire Cornelius Vanderbilt arranged for his ships to transport customers on two oceans. He used his own boats for river and lake travel in Nicaragua. Vanderbilt's ships were popular. However, the Panama route was preferred during the 1850s, when steamers could be hired instead of bungos, rates were cheaper, and cholera was no longer rampant.
10. Ferol Egan, *The El Dorado Trail: The Story of the Gold Rush Routes Across Mexico* (New York: McGraw-Hill, 1970), 231. A try kettle is a pot used on whalers to melt whale blubber.

CHAPTER 4. THE CAPE HORN ROUTE

1. New England ships frequently sailed around the tip of South America: whalers to fish Pacific waters; merchant vessels to trade for furs along the California coast and stop in China to buy tea and silks. As a result of the Gold Rush, many captains adapted their boats for passenger travel.
2. Oscar Lewis, *Sea Routes to the Gold Fields: The Migration by Water to California in 1849–1852* (New York: Alfred A. Knopf, 1949), 43.
3. Johnson, 52.
4. Lewis, *Sea Routes to the Gold Fields,* 109.
5. Groh, 67.
6. Langdon Sully, "General Sully Reports" in *American Heritage Magazine* (December 1964), 55.
7. Lewis, *Sea Routes to the Gold Fields,* 135.
8. *Ibid.,* 82.
9. *Robinson Crusoe* by Daniel Defoe (first published in 1719) was extremely popular during the nineteenth century. The idea of visiting an island that inspired this wonderful book excited the imagination of tourists to such an extent that some of them looked for Crusoe's footprints.

CHAPTER 5. OVERLAND

1. New Jersey's Newark Overland Company; the Charleston, Virginia, Mining Company; the Washington City Company; and many other groups from the East chose overland routes.
2. In 1846 the Donner party had been trapped in the mountains by an October snowfall. There is a legend that the Donner party murdered one another for food. This was not so. Those who were living sustained themselves on the flesh of those who were dead. Out of eighty-seven, forty died.
3. Bari, 76.
4. Walker D. Wyman, *California Emigrant Letters* (New York: Bookman Associates, 1952), 112, 59.
5. Alonzo Delano, *Life on the Plains and Among the Diggings* (New Canaan, Conn.: Readex Microprint, 1966), 46.

6. Emigrants were unduly frightened about the possibility of being murdered by Indians. In fact, Indians had more cause for concern: ". . . the emigrants killed Indians more frequently than they themselves were being killed in almost every migration year." John D. Unruh, Jr. *The Plains Across: The Overland Emigrants and the Trans-Mississippi West, 1840–60* (Champaign, Ill.: University of Illinois Press, 1979), 184.

7. Wyman, 64.

8. J. Goldsborough Bruff. *Gold Rush, The Journals, Drawings, and Other Papers of J. Goldsborough Bruff* (New York: Columbia University Press, 1949), 12.

9. Joseph Banks, *The Buckeye Rovers in the Gold Rush* (Athens, Ohio: Ohio University Press, 1965), 24.

10. The slaughter of buffalo had started years before the Gold Rush, when traders bought meat and skins from Indians. The artist George Catlin reported that in one instance, Sioux exchanged fourteen hundred buffalo tongues for a few gallons of whiskey. Buffalo robes were also in great demand.

11. The trail was so smooth that highway engineers used it to construct I-80.

12. Ralph Andrist, "Gold" in *American Heritage Magazine* (December 1962), 11. Delano quoted.

13. Elisha Douglass Perkins, *Gold Rush Diary: Being the Journal of Elisha Douglass Perkins on the Overland Trail in the Spring and Summer of 1849* (Lexington, Ky.: University of Kentucky Press, 1967), 30.

14. Delano, 86.

15. Holliday, 158.

16. One innovative doctor took advantage of the freezing weather. After milking two cows that pulled his wagon, he added peppermint oil from his medicine chest; because of the rough ride, the mixture became ice cream. (See Groh, 117.)

17. Caughey, 115–116.

18. Laurence I. Seidman, *The Fools of '49: The California Gold Rush 1848–1856* (New York: Alfred A. Knopf, 1976), 94.

19. R. C. Shaw, *Across the Plains in Forty-Nine,* quoted in note in Perkins, 120.

20. Banks, 88.

21. Death Valley is twice the size of the state of Delaware—some three thousand square miles of wasteland. It runs between mountain ranges for 140 miles, through Nevada and California.

22. Bruff, 151. A mirage is a trick of nature played upon the eyes. The reflection of the sky near the horizon can be mistaken for a distant lake, especially by those traveling through deserts.

23. Official report, quoted in notes in Bruff, 632.

24. Holliday, 175.

25. Southern routes were used by comparatively few, probably less than nine thousand. Tens of thousands took the midwest overland route. Historian John Unruh estimates that over two hundred thousand California-bound emigrants crossed the continent between 1849 and 1860. In addition, countless numbers traveled to California by ship. *There are no reliable statistics.*

26. Egan, 32.

27. Caughey, 131.

28. Egan, 92.

29. Some passengers returned home. Others formed small groups and made their way to California on their own. French surfaced in 1869 as a legislator for the California government.

CHAPTER 6. LAND OF PROMISE

1. Lewis, *Sutter's Fort,* 165.
2. Estimates vary because no one kept accurate records at that time.
3. In 1849, the year after San Francisco's two newspapers had been shut down because their staff had left for the mines, the *Alta California* newspaper was published in San Francisco. Subsequently many mining towns had their own newspapers.
4. Taylor, 85. This story about laundry being shipped to China and Hawaii seems hard to believe. Although it was reported by Taylor, some historians suspect that he may have neglected to verify it.
5. Perkins, 165 (Letter of Samuel Cross, Oct. 6, 1849).
6. The northern mines referred to the Feather, Yuba, Bear, and American rivers. The southern mines were located along the Cosumnes, Mokelumne, Calaveras, Stanislaus, Tuolumne, and Mariposa rivers.
7. Alonzo Delano, a prospector from Illinois, helped build two dams. One was never finished. The other cost sixteen thousand dollars to build and produced no gold. Delano wrote that several groups invested eight thousand dollars each building dams, and not one paid off.
8. Holliday, 350.

CHAPTER 7. THE DIGGINGS

1. Joseph Henry Jackson, *Anybody's Gold: The Story of California's Mining Towns* (San Francisco: Chronicle Books, 1970), 62.
2. "Bryant . . . has dug more gold than a mule can pack." Letter from M. T. McClellan, sent from San Francisco on Oct. 18, 1848. (See Wyman, 25.)
3. E. Gould Buffum in Bingham, 24.
4. Groh, 229.
5. Caughey, 169.
6. Groh, 232. Paden had pockets full of treasure, but his luck ran out. After six months in the gold fields, he became ill and died.
7. Dr. John Morse of Brooklyn and Dr. Jacob Stillman of Baltimore jointly opened a hospital in Sacramento in 1849. It was the finest hospital in the city.
8. Alexander Hamilton's son William, who crossed the plains and worked in the mines, died of cholera in August 1850. He was buried alongside other victims.
9. Wyman, 77–79.
10. Collis Huntington, Mark Hopkins, Charles Crocker, and Leland Stanford were to be known as "The Big Four" because they made fortunes financing the Central Pacific Railroad. Crocker, from Troy, New York, joined the Gold Rush in 1850. Stanford, also from Troy, New York, arrived in California in 1852. He founded Stanford University in 1861.

11. In 1851 J. Goldsborough Bruff was upset when a ten-hour fire destroyed his bedding. He was happy to rescue his diary from the flames. His diary is still a priceless source of information, enchanting to read.
12. Banks, 124.
13. J. Goldsborough Bruff named a man called Gibbs as the inventor of the Lake of Gold myth. Bruff intimated that Gibbs was in league with traders who profited by supplying the needs of hordes headed for the fabulous lake. (See Bruff, 701, 710.)
14. *Ibid.,* 473.
15. *Ibid.,* 726.

CHAPTER 8. LAW AND ORDER

1. Kevin Starr, *Americans and the California Dream 1850–1915* (New York: Oxford University Press, 1973), 56.
2. *Ibid.,* 56.
3. The Compromise of 1850 had the following provisions:
   -California was admitted as a free state.
   -A new Fugitive Slave Act would have stricter provisions for the return of runaway slaves.
   -The slavery issue was left undecided in the territories of New Mexico and Utah.
   -Slave trade was prohibited in the District of Columbia.
4. Holliday, 317.
5. Taylor, 71.
6. Caughey, 234.
7. E. Gould Buffum in Bingham, 25. This lynching changed the name of Dry Diggings to Hangtown, later to be changed to Placerville.
8. Louise Clappe, *The Shirley Letters* (Salt Lake City, Utah: Peregrine Smith Books, 1985), 85.
9. Constitution of the San Francisco Vigilance Committee
10. In 1856 another vigilante group was formed in San Francisco that claimed government justice was too slow. Charles Cora, who had killed a federal marshal, and James Case, who had killed a newspaper editor, were in jail awaiting trial. Vigilantes lynched and hanged them while thousands watched. Two other criminals were also hanged without being tried. The vigilantes disbanded after three months, and the government regained control.

CHAPTER 9. FOREIGNERS

1. Donald Dale Jackson, 291.
2. Stan Steiner, *Fusang: The Chinese Who Built America* (New York: Harper Colophon Books, 1979), 109.
3. *Ibid.,* 110.
4. Caughey, 230.
5. During the 1860s Chinese labor built the western part of the first transcontinental railroad. During the 1860s and 1870s thousands of Chinese also built whole or part of nearly every railroad line in the West.
6. Robert F. Heizer and Alan F. Almquist, *The Other Californians* (Berkeley and Los Angeles: University of California Press, 1977), 145.

7. Donald Dale Jackson, 288.
8. Holliday, 328.
9. James J. Rawls, *Indians of California: The Changing Image* (Norman, Okla.: University of Oklahoma Press, 1986), 124.
10. Holliday, 328.
11. Rawls, 141.
12. Seidman, 192.

CHAPTER 10. WOMEN

1. A forty-niner named Thissell wrote in his diary that when he heard that a woman had arrived at Snow's camp, he put on his best clothes and "struck out on foot to see the wonderful creature. . . . I walked 16 miles to see a woman in California." (See Seidman, 142.)
2. Lewis, *Sea Routes to the Gold Fields,* 30.
3. *Ibid.,* 31.
4. Donald Dale Jackson, 252. In 1854, Miss Sarah Pellet of California offered a plan similar to Mrs. Farnham's. She hoped to import five thousand females from New England. Each young lady's virtue would be guaranteed by the Sons of Temperance, the organization opposed to drinking hard liquor. Miss Pellet's plan failed because not enough women were willing to participate, and also because there were few Sons of Temperance in California.
5. Johnson, 131.
6. Lillian Schlissel, *Women's Diaries of the Westward Journey* (New York: Schocken Books, 1982), 61.
7. *Ibid.,* 64.
8. Clappe, 3. Mrs. Clappe's letters to her sister are an invaluable source of information about life in a mining camp.
9. *Ibid.,* 122.
10. *Ibid.,* 184.
11. Schlissel, 168.
12. On overland trails there was a constant fear that Indians might kidnap women and children. This was a very rare occurrence. On the Santa Fe trail, Apache Indians carried away a child named Olive Oatman, after having killed her parents, brother, and infant sister. Olive was sold to a Mohave tribe. Years later, pioneers found her, and took her away from the "savages." She tried to escape and return to her Indian husband and their children. To stop her, Olive was sent to relatives in Oregon. She subsequently married a banker from Texas. Tattoos on her face and body were reminders of her life as a Mohave woman. (See Schlissel, 69ff.)
13. In 1850 women were still a rarity: only 1 percent of the population. By the end of the 1850s the count increased to 30 percent. Most lived in cities; only 2 percent were at the diggings. (See Holliday, 352.)

CHAPTER 11. END OF THE RAINBOW

1. Arnold C. Brackman, *The Dream of Troy* (New York: Mason & Lipscomb, 1974), 60.
2. Lewis, *Sutter's Fort,* 176.

BIBLIOGRAPHY

PRIMARY SOURCES

Banks, Joseph. *The Buckeye Rovers in the Gold Rush.* Athens, Ohio: Ohio University Press, 1965.

Bari, Valeska. *The Course of Empire.* New York: Coward-McCann, 1931.

Bingham, Edwin. *California Gold, Selected Source Materials for College Research Papers.* Boston: Heath and Company, 1959. Contains excerpts from diaries: Colton, Walter, *Three Years in California;* Buck, Franklin A., *A Yankee Trader in the Gold Rush;* Buffum, E. Gould, *Six Months in the Gold Mines.*

Bruff, J. Goldsborough. *Gold Rush, The Journals, Drawings, and Other Papers of J. Goldsborough Bruff.* New York: Columbia University Press, 1949.

Clappe, Louise. *The Shirley Letters.* Salt Lake City, Utah: Peregrine Smith Books, 1985.

Delano, Alonzo. *Life on the Plains and Among the Diggings.* New Canaan, Conn.: Readex Microprint, 1966.

Holliday, J. S. *The World Rushed In: The California Gold Rush Experience.* New York: Simon & Schuster, 1981.

Perkins, Elisha Douglass. *Gold Rush Diary: Being the Journal of Elisha Douglass Perkins on the Overland Trail in the Spring and Summer of 1849.* Lexington, Ky.: University of Kentucky Press, 1967.

Perlot, Jean-Nicolas. *Gold Seeker: Adventures of a Belgian Argonaut During the Gold Rush Years.* New Haven, Conn.: Yale University Press, 1985.

Schlissel, Lillian. *Women's Diaries of the Westward Journey.* New York: Schocken Books, 1982. Includes "A Woman's Trip Across the Plains in 1849" (diary of Catherine Haun).

Simpson, Henry. *Three Weeks in the Gold Mines, or Adventures with the Diggers of California Gold.* New York: Joyce & Co., 1848.

Taylor, Bayard. *Eldorado or Adventures in the Path of Empire.* New York: Alfred A. Knopf, 1949.

Ware, Joseph E. *The Emigrants' Guide to California.* (Reprint of 1849 edition.) New York: Da Capo Press, 1972.

Wienpahl, Robert W., ed. *A Gold Rush Voyage on the Bark Orion.* Glendale, Calif.: Arthur H. Clark Co., 1978.

Wyman, Walker D. *California Emigrant Letters.* New York: Bookman Associates, 1952.

SECONDARY SOURCES

Andrist, Ralph. "Gold." *American Heritage Magazine* (December 1962).

Bean, Walton. *California, An Interpretive History.* New York: McGraw-Hill, 1968.

Brackman, Arnold C. *The Dream of Troy.* New York: Mason & Lipscomb, 1974.

Caughey, John Walton. *The California Gold Rush.* Berkeley and Los Angeles: University of California Press, 1973.

Egan, Ferol. *The El Dorado Trail: The Story of the Gold Rush Routes Across Mexico.* New York: McGraw-Hill, 1970.

Groh, George W. *Gold Fever: Being a True Account, Both Horrifying and Hilarious of the Art of Healing (so-called) During the California Gold Rush.* New York: William Morrow, 1966.

Heizer, Robert F., and Alan F. Almquist, *The Other Californians.* Berkeley and Los Angeles: University of California Press, 1977.

Hoexter, Corrine K. *From Canton to California, The Epic of Chinese Immigration.* New York: Four Winds Press, 1976.

Jackson, Donald Dale. *Gold Dust.* Lincoln, Nebr.: University of Nebraska Press, 1980.

Jackson, Joseph Henry. *Anybody's Gold: The Story of California's Mining Towns.* San Francisco: Chronicle Books, 1970.

Johnson, William Weber. *The Forty-Niners.* Alexandria, Va.: Time-Life Books, 1974.

Lapp, Rudolph M. *Blacks in the Gold Rush.* New Haven: Yale University Press, 1977.

Lewis, Oscar. *Sea Routes to the Gold Fields: The Migration by Water to California in 1849–1852.* New York: Alfred A. Knopf, 1949.

————. *Sutter's Fort: Gateway to the Gold Fields.* Englewood Cliffs, N.J.: Prentice-Hall, 1966.

Rawls, James J. *Indians of California: The Changing Image.* Norman, Okla.: University of Oklahoma Press, 1986.

Seidman, Laurence I. *The Fools of '49: The California Gold Rush 1848–1856.* New York: Alfred A. Knopf, 1976.

Starr, Kevin. *Americans and the California Dream 1850–1915.* New York: Oxford University Press, 1973.

Steiner, Stan. *Fusang: The Chinese Who Built America.* New York: Harper Colophon Books, 1979.

Sully, Langdon. "General Sully Reports." *American Heritage Magazine* (December 1964).

Unruh, John D., Jr. *The Plains Across: The Overland Emigrants and the Trans-Mississippi West, 1840–60.* Champaign, Ill.: University of Illinois Press, 1979.

White, Stewart S. *The Forty-Niners,* New Haven, Conn.: Yale University Press, 1921.

INDEX

Illustration references are in **boldface type.**

RHODA BLUMBERG has been acclaimed for her masterful presentations of landmark events in history. The opening of Japan (1853–1854) is covered in *Commodore Perry in the Land of the Shogun,* a 1986 Newbery Honor Book, which also won the Boston Globe/Horn Book Award and the Golden Kite Award.

The Incredible Journey of Lewis and Clark, about the famed expedition (1804–1806), is an ALA Notable Book and also a Golden Kite Award-winner. *School Library Journal*'s starred review of the book said that the author "shines in the imaginative use of extensive research to tell, compellingly and entertainingly, stories from history," and ALA *Booklist*'s starred review noted, "rarely has the expedition been so humanized as under Blumberg's fluent pen."